UK Parties & Pressure Groups

Neil Smith

Advanced
Topic*Master*

Series editor
Eric Magee

For Rebecca, Alice, Mollie and Rosy

Philip Allan Updates
Market Place
Deddington
Oxfordshire
OX15 0SE

Orders
Bookpoint Ltd, 130 Milton Park, Abingdon, Oxfordshire, OX14 4SB
tel: 01235 827720
fax: 01235 400454
e-mail: uk.orders@bookpoint.co.uk
Lines are open 9.00 a.m.–5.00 p.m., Monday to Saturday, with a 24-hour message answering service. You can also order through the Philip Allan Updates website: www.philipallan.co.uk

© Philip Allan Updates 2007

ISBN 978-1-84489-646-2

Printed in Spain

Philip Allan Updates' policy is to use papers that are natural, renewable and recyclable products and made from wood grown in sustainable forests. The logging and manufacturing processes are expected to conform to the environmental regulations of the country of origin.

P00947

Contents

Introduction

Both political parties and pressure groups have a special role in modern forms of democracy. The current interpretation of representative democracy is based on the idea that the electorate votes for a package of policies and symbols associated with a particular party, and in the process provides the winning party with a mandate to govern. However, recent years have seen both the popularity of political parties and voter turnout decline, as voters have questioned the point of supporting parties that offer few points of difference between them, and have increasingly questioned the effectiveness of the electoral system in delivering a fair result. Some commentators believe that political activity has changed to the extent that they regard campaign groups as more representative of their beliefs and more democratic in their internal organisation.

In many ways, this change represents the underlying theme of the book: to what extent are traditional forms of politics in decline, and why? Chapter 1 considers the alleged decline of the two-party system, and examines the case for the emergence for a multitude of party systems in the UK. Chapter 2 is concerned with the ideological backgrounds of the major parties, and explores the evidence for the existence for a new consensus. The extent to which parties are internally democratic is the focus of Chapter 3, where I attempt to reconcile the apparent increase in member democracy with claims that modern parties have become professional electoral machines with little need of loyal members. Chapter 4 looks at the different types of pressure group and explains emerging trends in pressure group behaviour. The final chapter focuses on the contribution that pressure groups make to the workings of democracy.

Parties and pressure groups cover almost all forms of popular participation in British politics. Even if individuals do not belong to either a party or a group, it is highly likely that they will have voted for one of them, or performed some act, such as signing a petition, or making a donation which demonstrates a degree of sympathy with their goals. In essence, therefore, this book is about the opportunities we have to participate in politics, and how we choose to exploit them.

For easy reference, terms that are defined in the glossary are highlighted in purple the first time they appear.

Neil Smith

Do we now have multiparty politics?

Most descriptions of the British political system refer to the existence of a *two-party system* within the first few paragraphs. It is taken as a given that the dominance of Labour and Conservatives is what has been, what is and what will always be. The evidence for this assertion is not hard to find; simply consider which parties have formed the government since 1945, which parties get the overwhelming majority of votes, and which parties are able to win seats nationwide.

However, recent events have given rise to a belief that the British party system is undergoing a profound transformation, with the extent and depth of support for the two main parties in decline, and a dispersal of votes to a range of other parties. Indeed, some commentators have argued that the two-party era is over, and that an age of multiparty politics is upon us.

By examining the nature of different party systems, and discussing the origins and nature of the British party system, this chapter explores how far the old assumptions about the British party system are still accurate, and whether we now need to discuss the structure of British party politics in a different fashion.

Does the nature of our party system matter?

Throughout the Western world, no single party system dominates. Most states have one of the following types of party system.

One-party system

Two main types of one-party state exist. Type A, usually to be found in Communist states, guarantees the ruling status of the party in a constitution, and all forms of political opposition are banned by law. The ruling party controls all aspects of life in that state, e.g. Cuba, North Korea.

Type B originates from broader independence movements, which unite in the post-colonial era to form a single party. Multiparty elections may still be held, but no other party is either able or allowed to take over the reins of office, e.g. Zimbabwe, Ghana.

Two-party system

This is a system in which just two parties dominate, e.g. UK, USA. Other parties may exist but they have no political importance. For the system to work, one of the parties must obtain a sufficient working majority after an election and it must be in a position to be able to govern without the support of the other party. A rotation of power is expected in this system, i.e. both major parties are electable, and when not in office, they act as the principal source of opposition to the government.

Multiparty system

As the title suggests, this is a system in which more than two parties have some impact on national political life, e.g. Germany. It could be argued that the UK is slowly evolving into a multiparty state; although the Labour Party has a healthy majority in Westminster, its power in the regions is much weaker because of the strength of several rival parties in the devolutionary structure.

Dominant-party system

This is different from a one-party system, and exists, for example, in India and Japan. Within the political structure of a state, a party can become dominant to such an extent that electoral victory over a prolonged period of time is considered a formality. The big question though is: how long is a prolonged period? Should the Conservative governments of Margaret Thatcher and John Major (1979–97) be considered an era of dominant-party rule? Perhaps better examples are found in Japan, where the Liberal Democratic Party ruled from 1955 until 1993, or in India, where the Congress Party has been out of office for only 12 years between 1947 and 2006.

Learning point

How do you work out what type of party system a country has?

Consider the following criteria which could be used to decide what kind of party system exists in a particular country. Which are the most important in deciding the number of significant parties?

- number of votes a party receives in an election
- number of seats a party receives in an election
- a party's ability to govern alone
- a party's 'blackmail' potential (i.e. when a smaller coalition partner holds the balance of power)
- coalition potential

Why does the type of party system matter?

For most people living under these different party systems, political life differs very little; they live in liberal democracies, with regular elections and constituency-based representation.

It sends out a message about the country

Some scholars argue that the shift from voting for people who possessed a hold over individuals (e.g. landowners or tribal leaders) to voting for parties offering alternative platforms, often based around abstract ideas, marked a significant turning point in the development of political society. In this way, the development of a party system could be viewed as an essential step in the development of a democratic system.

Weaker party systems may encourage the rise of anti-party, and possibly anti-democratic, politicians

Mainwaring and Torcal (2001) argue that the critical role political parties play in providing electoral accountability is undermined if a strong party system does not exist. They suggest that in systems where parties frequently come and go, or where charismatic individuals dominate the political process, effective electoral accountability suffers as a result of the absence of established alternatives.

It may influence the nature of political competition

A political system that has a higher number of *relevant* political parties involves a much greater degree of bartering and compromise between the executive and the legislature. This is mainly because multiparty systems tend to be found in countries where a *proportional* system of voting is used, and therefore no single party is likely to be able to govern single-handedly.

Two-party systems tend to create a heavily contested centre ground, because there is no real incentive to move towards the edges of the political spectrum for fear of losing a large number of moderate voters to the other party in the duopoly. It could be argued that both major parties in Britain today distinguish themselves from each other mainly on the grounds of competence, rather than ideas.

Does Britain have a two-party system?

In his 1955 work, *British Political Parties*, Robert McKenzie argued that political competition in Britain took place in the context of a two-party system. The two-party system operated on three levels: first, who dominated the House of Commons; second, who formed the government; and finally, who received the bulk of votes cast.

As Table 1.1 suggests, Britain's electoral history from the end of Second World War until the mid-1970s would appear to strongly bear out McKenzie's thesis.

Table 1.1 British general election results, 1945–February 1974

Election	Combined Labour and Conservative MPs	Party which formed the government	Combined percentage vote for Labour and Conservative
1945	603/640	Labour	88
1950	613/625	Labour	85
1951	616/625	Conservative	97
1955	622/630	Conservative	91
1959	623/630	Conservative	89
1964	620/629	Labour	84
1966	605/629	Labour	87
1970	609/629	Conservative	87
February 1974	597/634	Labour	74

Note: The number of Conservative seats 1945–64 includes those won by their political associates, such as Ulster Unionists, Conservative and National Liberals, National Liberal and Conservative, Conservative and Liberal, Liberal and Conservative, and National Liberal.

Source: www.psr.keele.ac.uk/area/uk/edates.htm

As Table 1.1 indicates, from 1945 until February 1974, the Conservative and Labour parties completely dominated the electoral landscape, enjoying over 80% of the vote and an overwhelming majority of seats in the House of Commons.

Chapter 1

However, one could make the case that McKenzie's argument is not supported simply by evidence from this 30-year period. The results of subsequent general elections could also support his position:

- No other party, apart from Labour or the Conservatives, has gained a majority in the House of Commons. Indeed, no other party has won a 'second-order' election in Britain (i.e. an election that does not affect the composition of the government and is regarded as less important than a general election).
- The distribution of power between the two main parties remains roughly equal. Since 1945, the Conservatives have held office for 35 years, while Labour has done so for 26 years.
- As Table 1.2 shows, both parties' shares of the vote and parliamentary seats remain high.

Table 1.2 Labour and Conservative share of the vote and parliamentary seats, 1992–2005

Election	Labour and Conservative share of the vote (%)	Labour and Conservative share of parliamentary seats (%)
1992	76	92
1997	74	88
2001	73	78
2005	68	85

- The share of the vote between the main parties is broadly similar. In the 'golden age' of the two-party system, Labour and Conservative both regularly polled over 40% of the total vote, with the gap between them never exceeding 8%, and averaging out at approximately 3%. In 2001, the gap was 8%, but in 2005 it narrowed to 3%.
- As well as winning most of the seats they contest, the two main parties are also most likely to come second in a constituency. Labour came either first or second in 495 of the 627 constituencies, while the Conservatives came either first or second in 467 of the 630 constituencies in which they stood. (This total includes three constituencies in Northern Ireland, where the Conservatives fielded candidates.)
- Meanwhile, no likely challenge to the two-party system appears credible. Support for the Liberal Democrats remains below 25%, even though it did increase by 3% in 2005.

The causes of Britain's two-party system are many and varied

The class-based nature of British political parties

This has influenced the development of a two-party system in two ways. First, class has traditionally been the dominant factor in determining voters' attitudes to political parties, and we should not therefore be surprised to see voters opting for the 'natural' parties of the working and middle classes (Table 1.3).

Table 1.3 Occupational class of 'head of household' and party choice, 1964–74

	1964		1970		1974	
	Non-manual (%)	Manual (%)	Non-manual (%)	Manual (%)	Non-manual (%)	Manual (%)
Conservative	62	28	61	25	63	33
Labour	22	64	26	69	26	58
Liberal Democrat	15	8	26	69	26	58
Other					2	2

Source: British Election Study 1964–70, reproduced from D. Denver (2003) *Elections and Voters in Britain*.

Second, having found their 'natural' political home, voters are reluctant to abandon it for pastures new. Strong levels of party identification have helped perpetuate the duopoly in the British party system. With a relatively stable electorate, 'other' parties have inevitably found it difficult to break up the Labour–Conservative hegemony.

The impact of single-member plurality (SMP)

The most famous exponent of the link between electoral systems and party systems is Maurice Duverger. He argued that single-ballot 'winner takes all' elections, such as those held in the UK under single-member plurality (SMP), lead to the emergence of a two-party system. He argued that SMP penalises parties with similar ideological positions when faced with a common political enemy. His argument is essentially based on common sense: if there are 50,000 voters in a constituency, faced with a choice between two parties with conservative leanings and a third, with a more socialist position, the conservative vote may well be split, allowing the socialists to win the seat. As a result, the two conservative parties would have to merge if they wanted to prevent further socialist victories.

The effect on third or fourth parties is exaggerated as a result of the mechanical effects of SMP. This is sometimes referred to as the 'cube law'. This states that the relationship between votes and seats won is not directly proportional, but wholly disproportional. Roughly speaking, once a party has received a certain percentage of the vote, say 40%, then each percentage point won equates to more than 1% increase in seats won.

Duverger also claimed that the mechanical effects of SMP are compounded by a *psychological* effect on voters. If they know that no other party is likely to win a seat, other than the Labour or Conservative, they are likely to feel disinclined to vote for a third party.

The logical deduction therefore is that there is little incentive for any rival parties to emerge which share the same ideological position of either Labour or the Conservatives.

Other studies, while broadly agreeing with Duverger's line of argument, have pointed to the greater significance of single-member constituencies being a decisive factor in determining the shape of party systems around the world. Taagepera and Shugart (1989) suggest that the two-party system is the exception rather than the rule in countries that contain multi-member constituencies, even when a plurality voting system (such as 'first past the post', FPTP), is used. Applying this argument to the UK, the existence of single-member constituencies is therefore more likely to produce a two-party system.

Task 1.1

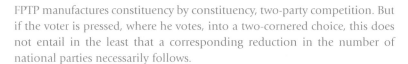

> FPTP manufactures constituency by constituency, two-party competition. But if the voter is pressed, where he votes, into a two-cornered choice, this does not entail in the least that a corresponding reduction in the number of national parties necessarily follows.
>
> Sartori (1997) *Comparative Constitutional Engineering*

(a) Explain the main reason why Giovanni Sartori does not believe that Duverger's Law is necessarily correct.

(b) Using your own knowledge, what evidence is there that the results of the 2005 general election support Sartori's position?

Guidance

(a) Essentially, Sartori argues that unless competition between two particular parties at constituency level is replicated across the country, there is no automatic reason why FPTP should lead to the development of a two-party system.

(b) First, the distribution of the seats in Northern Ireland and Scotland offers some evidence to support this viewpoint, even though the situation in these two regions is somewhat different from that in the rest of the UK. Second, the Liberal Democrats' performance in specific parts of the country such as the South West and the North West, and their ability to win seats from Labour and the Conservatives, would also add weight to Sartori's argument. However, overall, the picture which emerges is that of a weakened, but essentially stable, two-party system. At no point since the Second World War has the number of seats won by both main parties fallen below 80%; no other party has the reach and depth of support to win seats throughout the country; both Labour and Conservatives frequently come second in seats which they do not win.

The centralised nature of the British political system

Where political systems divide power more equally between central and regional authorities, multiparty systems tend to dominate. This may be due to the existence of powerful locally based parties, or because a party with a strong regional organisation and profile may find it easier to win seats nationally. Until 1997, power in the UK resided almost entirely in Westminster, thus making it difficult for any party without a genuine national presence to achieve credible electoral success. After 1997, a process of devolution provided new opportunities for regional parties to break through.

Political consensus

Unfortunately for the Liberal Democrats and their earlier manifestations, both major parties have achieved decades of electoral success on the back of co-opting mainly liberal ideas. In the post-war era, the interventionist ideas of 'New' Liberals formed the basis of the Keynesian consensus, but since the late 1970s, the beliefs of another strand of liberalism have underpinned a more market-based consensus. With the Labour and Conservative parties adapting many of their ideas, the Liberal Democrats have found it difficult to present a meaningful case for change.

Tight party organisation

Since any cracks in Britain's two-party system are likely to occur when a new political force emerges, the strength of the Labour and Conservative organisations could be seen as a further explanation for the maintenance of their duopoly.

A tightly organised party is one in which defections among its leadership are rare. Defections could involve party leaders leaving either to join another party or to form a new political party.

The strength in this argument could be illustrated by the most serious challenge to the dominance of the 'big two' since 1945. In 1980, four senior members of the Labour Party left to set up the Social Democratic Party (SDP) — a party intent on 'breaking the mould of British politics'. After a few high-profile by-election successes, the SDP came close to reshaping Britain's party system in the 1983 general election. Not only did the party receive 25% of the vote, compared with Labour's 28%, it also came second in 313 seats. Labour came second in 132 and third or worse in 292 constituencies.

However, in terms of actual seats won, the SDP's returns were less encouraging, as it won only 23 seats, compared with Labour's total of 209. Labour retained its position as the second party, albeit one incapable of offering a serious alternative to the Conservatives until many years later.

Where is the two-party system going?

McKenzie's description of Britain's party system could also be described as initially simplistic and of little relevance in the modern age.

First, it relied on a generalisation of the political situation across the whole of the UK, so it ignored significant regional 'micro-systems'. In several parts of the country, the main political competition was not between Labour and Conservative, but between one of the main parties and either a regional rival (e.g. Scottish National Party or Plaid Cymru) or the Liberals/Liberal Democrats. In 2005, the Liberal Democrats were the nearest challengers in 189 seats, with intense local rivalries giving the impression of genuine three-party politics in certain areas of the UK. Particular parts of the UK could also be said to have a *dominant*-party system, with no real competition being provided by any rival party. This is illustrated in Figure 1.1.

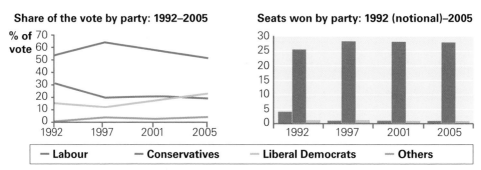

Figure 1.1 Share of the vote in the North East, general elections, 1992–2005
Source: House of Commons Library Research Paper 05/33

Second, McKenzie's thesis fails to account for the diverse political situations in Scotland and Wales since the mid-1970s. In both cases, the Conservatives have struggled to win seats, while the Liberal Democrats and respective nationalist parties have arguably created a mini multiparty system (Table 1.4).

Table 1.4 Result of the 2005 general election in Scotland

	Share of the vote (%)	Number of seats
Conservative	15.8	1
Labour	38.9	40
Liberal Democrats	22.6	11
SNP	17.7	6

Source: D. Denver (2005) 'Four-party competition in Scotland', *Politics Review*, Vol. 15, No. 2

Third, McKenzie ignores the unique situation that exists in Northern Ireland. Of the main UK parties, only the Conservatives entered candidates in the province. (In 2005, they stood in three constituencies.) Party loyalties are influenced more by religious or cultural factors in Northern Ireland, and while there are two clearly recognisable *communities*, competition tends to be within, rather than against, each community. As a result, the division of seats resembles more closely that of a multiparty system, rather than a traditional two-party system (Table 1.5).

Table 1.5 Result of the 2005 general election in Northern Ireland

	Share of the vote (%)	Number of seats	Change from 2001
Democratic Unionist Party	34	9	+4
Ulster Unionist Party	18	1	−5
Sinn Fein	24	5	+1
Social Democratic and Labour Party	18	3	0

Source: http://news.bbc.co.uk/1/shared/vote2005/html/region_6.stm

Fourth, if we consider the performance of parties in local, regional and European elections, a more complex, and arguably more interesting, picture emerges. At a local level, it is impossible to deploy a single term to describe the varied political situations throughout England and Wales. For example, while Stockport Council appears to have a multiparty system, the neighbouring council in Macclesfield is a prime example of a dominant party system. Not only do the Conservatives enjoy a healthy 12-seat overall majority, but they have been the ruling party since 1976. In regional and European Parliament elections, voters have exploited the opportunities presented by proportional methods of voting to switch their allegiance from the main parties to smaller parties, thus creating multiparty competition in parts of the UK.

Fifth, electoral support for the two main parties has fallen considerably since the era that McKenzie was describing. A quick comparison of the figures from 1951 and 2005 makes this point clearly. As indicated earlier, 97% of voters cast their vote for the two main parties in 1951, but in 2005, only 68% were willing to do so. Table 1.2 confirms that this was not an isolated result.

Task 1.2

Study the following items carefully, and answer the questions that follow.

Item A

Luke Smith (centre) was one of eight BNP councillors elected in Burnley in 2003. They became the official opposition on the council.

Item B London Assembly results, 2004

Party	Seats
Conservative	9
Labour	7
Liberal Democrats	5
UKIP	2
Green	2

Task 1.2 (continued)

Item C Elections to the European Parliament results, 2004

	Share of the vote	Number of seats (%)
Conservative	26.7	27
Labour	22.6	19
UKIP	16.1	12
Lib Dem	14.9	12
Green	6.3	2
BNP	4.9	0
Respect	1.5	0
SNP	1.4	2
PC	1.0	1
SSP	0.4	0
Other	4.6	3

Source: *BBC Online*, June 2004

Item D

Dr Richard Taylor won the seat of Wyre Forest in 2001 and 2005, standing as an Independent candidate against the closure of a local hospital. His success followed on from that of Martin Bell in 1997 in Tatton.

Richard Taylor

(a) In what ways do Items A–D suggest that we have multiparty politics in the UK?

(b) How could you challenge that argument?

Task 1.2 (continued)

Guidance

(a) Items A–D suggest that beyond Westminster a greater range of parties is able to gain a significant number of seats. It would also demonstrate that voters are prepared to cast their votes in a more diverse way when the electoral system allows them to (e.g. in the European Parliament elections), which one might expect to be a precondition of a multiparty system. Finally, the success of Martin Bell and Richard Taylor in general elections, and the BNP at local level, indicates that voter attachment to the main parties has weakened considerably: to the extent that they are willing to vote for 'anti-party' candidates.

(b) In each of the elections referred to in Items A–D, either the winner or second-placed candidate was one of the 'big two', with the winning party in the general, European, local and London assembly elections being either Labour or the Conservative Party. No other party has demonstrated either sufficient permanent achievement or the ability to do well in all types of election to justify any kind of reference to the term 'multiparty' politics.

What factors have contributed to the weakening of the two-party system?

British political parties becoming less class-based

It should be remembered that McKenzie was writing during a 'golden era' of class alignment. As indicated earlier, voters predominantly followed their class instincts in elections, and as the class system itself remained intact, there was little reason to believe that any change to the structure of Britain's party system was likely. However, since the mid-1970s, both major parties have experienced significant changes in the extent and strength of support from their natural supporters. Less than half of the electorate now vote for the party which traditionally represents their class interests, while the number of voters who could be said to strongly identify with a party is less than 20%.

The impact of these processes on the party system has been profound. Although there has been no serious challenge to the main parties' ability to win general elections, there has been a serious leakage of votes to minor parties in several recent elections.

The impact of the electoral system

The consequences of this leakage of votes have largely been camouflaged by the prejudices of the electoral system. However, the system's ability to deny representation to minor parties has been undermined in recent elections as voters and parties have realised the opportunities that single-member plurality provides for *tactical voting*. Voters have demonstrated an increased willingness to 'gang up' on individual parties, with the usual victim being one of the two main parties. As a result, minor parties such as the Liberal Democrats have been able to triple their share of seats without a proportional increase in their share of the vote (Table 1.6).

| Table 1.6 | Liberal Democrat votes and seats, 1992–2005 |

	Share of the vote (%)	Number of seats (share of seats %)
1992	17.8	20 (3.1)
1997	16.8	46 (7.0)
2001	18.3	52 (7.9)
2005	22.0	62 (9.6)

Source: House of Commons Library Research Paper 05/33

Challenges to the two-party system have also emerged out of the new electoral systems introduced for the devolved assemblies and the European elections. Duverger is not alone in suggesting that proportional electoral systems tend to create multiparty systems. In her study of the impact of electoral systems and party systems, Pippa Norris (1994) highlighted the differing impacts of electoral systems on party systems. By focusing on the number of relevant parties (those obtaining more than 3% of the parliamentary seats) that emerge in legislatures under different types of electoral system, she confirmed Duverger's theory.

The explanation for the higher number of relevant parliamentary parties is not simply mechanical. One can also assume that voters are aware that their votes will not be wasted to the same extent as they are under SMP, so they are therefore more willing to cast them in the direction of smaller parties.

The consequences of the use of proportional representation (PR) in the UK since 1997 for the number of effective parties are shown in Figure 1.2.

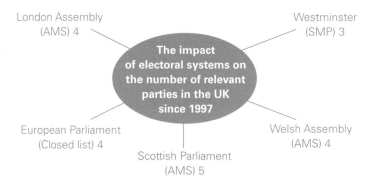

Figure 1.2 Impact of the electoral system in the UK
(AMS = additional member system)

Source: The Constitution Unit, *Changed Voting Changed Politics:
Lessons of Britain's Experience of PR Since 1997*, April 2003

Additionally, in neither Scotland nor Wales has Labour been able to govern without the need to rely on a coalition partner. (After the 2003 elections, the Welsh Labour group decided to govern alone, even though it did not have an overall majority of assembly members.)

Learning point

Most academics agree that proportional electoral systems in other countries produce a higher number of relevant parliamentary parties than those parts of the UK where PR is used.

Why do you think the number of relevant parliamentary parties after PR elections is lower in the UK?

Disillusionment with the Big Two

Disillusionment with Britain's traditional ruling parties is demonstrated clearly by their performance in the 2005 election. While Labour won the election with only 35% of the vote (a figure below their *losing* total in 1979), their nearest rivals could muster only 32% of the vote. This hardly seems to be a case of two political heavyweights destroying everything in their path. Why should this be the case?

If voters feel less strongly attached to political parties, then perhaps we should also expect them to be more critical of their record in and out of office. Both parties have suffered electorally when they have strayed away from the centre ground of British politics. In 1983, Labour paid for its lurch leftwards by recording its worst result since before the Second World War, and in the process almost allowed the new SDP–Liberal Alliance to replace it as the second party in Britain. Similarly, the Conservatives' inability to improve on their 1997 meltdown, in percentage terms at least, is partially attributable to their failure to broaden their outlook beyond those policies which instinctively play well with their core supporters.

Recent elections have suggested that an apparent lack of choice between the two parties has driven voters away. This has allowed UK Independence Party and the Greens to pick up votes in European and London elections, and is a likely contributory factor to the increase in support for the British National Party (BNP) in local elections.

How should we describe the UK party system in the twenty-first century?

Do we still have a two-party system?

It is increasingly difficult to describe party politics in Britain as a two-party system. Popular support for the two largest parties is in decline, in all forms of elections, and an extensive range of smaller parties have also demonstrated an ability to pick up seats from both Labour and Conservative since 1997. So, if it is not a *two-party* system, what is it?

Do we have a dominant-party system?

The case for

- After the fourth Conservative election win in a row in 1992, academics suggested that Britain was entering a new political era, with a two-party system being supplanted by one where a single party, the Conservatives, dominated. The 1992 election was significant because it marked the first time since the Second World War that a party had gone beyond three consecutive elections. Conservative dominance was further demonstrated by the decline in support for the Liberal Democrats, suggesting that there was little hope of a new centrist party simply replacing Labour in a new two-party system. What made the Conservatives' achievement especially remarkable was that they had won four elections in economic conditions that were not always conducive to incumbent victory.

- The crushing electoral defeat suffered by the Conservatives in 1997 would, at first glance, appear to shatter any claims for the existence of a dominant-party system. However, if we consider not only Labour's three election victories, but also the scale of victory in 1997 and 2001, alongside a comfortable majority in 2005, and then note the party's victories in the Scottish and Welsh regional elections, then perhaps there is cause for claiming that Labour has replaced the Conservatives as the dominant party in British politics.
- Some might claim that Labour's sequence of victories actually confirms Conservative political supremacy. Even though the Conservative Party has lost its dominant position, its *ideas* still dominate British politics, albeit through a Labour government which has had to adopt Conservative economic and social policies in order to regain power.

The case against

- Compared with other countries that are frequently held up as models of a dominant-party system, Britain has experienced comparatively short periods of single-party dominance. In Japan, the Liberal Democratic Party was in power from 1955 to 1993, and in Sweden, the Social Democratic Labour Party was able to rule alone, or with the help of smaller coalition partners, for all but 2 years from 1951 to 1993. Neither of the main UK parties has been close to either of these examples.
- Although the Conservatives managed to preserve a reputation as an awesome seat-accumulating machine, as Table 1.7 shows, their dominance was not reflected in their share of the vote.

Table 1.7 Conservative share of the vote in UK general elections, 1979–92

Year	Share (%)
1979	43.87
1983	42.44
1987	42.23
1992	41.93

- Even during their periods of supposed supremacy, neither the Conservatives or Labour could claim to be a genuine national party. The Conservatives struggled to make any electoral impact in Scotland, Wales and a large section of the north of England, while Labour relies on its support in Scotland and Wales to hold onto power — the Conservatives being the largest party in England. A quick glance at the electoral map of England after 2005 highlights this point and suggests that there are large parts of England that remain an electoral wasteland for the party.

- In spite of its success in general elections, Labour has not been able to assert its dominance in all electoral arenas. Following the 2003 devolution elections, it has been forced to govern in partnership with the Liberal Democrats in Scotland, and in Wales only as a minority government. In both sets of elections to the European Parliament since 1997, Labour has been forced into second place by the Conservatives — something which the Conservatives themselves only suffered after being in power for 10 years.

Do we have a three-party system?

The case for

- The Liberal Democrats' total of 62 MPs in 2005 was an increase of 11 on their 2001 figure, and the highest total for a third party since the Liberal Party won 158 seats in 1923.
- The Liberal Democrats have also established themselves as the second party in 189 constituencies. In the South West, they replaced Labour as the second party in the region, increasing both their share of the vote and number of seats won. They are also the second party in Wales and Scotland, and came a close third place in the London Assembly elections.
- In local government, the Liberal Democrats have staked a claim for genuine three-party politics. In 2006, the party managed to push Labour into third place, although it won fewer seats than Labour. The Liberal Democrats currently hold just 4,700 council seats, compared with 8,482 held by the Conservatives and 6,164 by Labour.

The case against

- The Liberal Democrats have failed to achieve a share of the vote as high as that enjoyed by the SDP–Liberal Alliance in 1983 and 1987.
- Evidence from 2005 lends weight to the case that the depth of support for the Liberal Democrats is shallow. In seats that they won in 1997, their support fell by 2.0% and in those which they took in 2001, support fell by 1.9%. This does not suggest growing momentum.
- Their overall increase in the share of the vote was chiefly due to their ability to win support in seats which Labour had won in 1997 and 2001. They were unable to maintain this advance on two fronts though, with only a small increase in votes in seats held by the Conservatives. As a result, this suggests that they remain at best an outlet for voters disillusioned with the performance of one of the two main parties.

Do we have a multiparty system?

The case for

- The main argument in favour of a multiparty system is that the number of relevant parties in non-Westminster elections, and in general elections in Scotland, is markedly higher than would be expected in a conventional two-party system. As indicated above, the number of relevant parliamentary parties in these elections is four or above; in some elections, at least one of the parties is not currently represented in parliament. This evidence might suggest that only the continued use of SMP is preventing the emergence of a multiparty system in parliament.

- As the Conservative and Labour share of the vote has fallen in general elections, so the share of the vote enjoyed by a range of minor parties has risen. The key point is that no single party was the sole beneficiary from the decline in support for the two main parties. The improvement in the Liberal Democrats' performance has already been noted, but in Scotland, the SNP polled more than the Conservatives in 2005, gained 2 seats, and was the second-place party in 19 further seats. Interestingly, no SNP candidate has lost his/her deposit in a general election since 1987. In practice, that means that the party has gained more than the 5% threshold for keeping the deposit in each seat which it has contested. In Wales, Plaid Cymru's performance could offer further evidence of a break-up of the two-party system. The party gained its first and second highest share of the vote in its history in 2001 (14.3%) and 2005 (12.6%). Smaller parties performed well in England as well. Dr Richard Taylor (Independent Kidderminster Hospital and Health Concern) retained his seat in Wyre Forest, while George Galloway's Respect–Unity Coalition took Bethnal Green and Bow from Labour in a high-profile and vicious campaign, and finished second in four other seats in London and Birmingham.

The case against

- The strongest argument against the idea that Britain now has a multiparty system is that no other party has been able to make the necessary electoral breakthrough in Westminster elections. Even when disillusion with the major parties was at its highest point since the Second World War, the Liberal Democrats failed to replace the Conservatives as the main opposition party, and only three 'other' parties were able to win a seat. In each case, local factors played a decisive part in the result. Neither the Greens nor UKIP, two parties that have won seats in previous non-Westminster elections, could achieve higher than third place in any of the constituencies that they fought.

- Any claim that the UK has a multiparty system which bases its argument on the growth of the SNP as an electoral force in Westminster elections must be treated with some caution. Although the SNP's share of the seats increased from 4 to 6, the party actually received its lowest share of the vote in Scotland since 1987, obtaining 17.7% of the vote. (In 2001 the SNP won 20.1%.)

Conclusion

As the above analysis suggests, what McKenzie identified as a stable two-party system in the 1950s has all but disappeared. But what has replaced it? Unfortunately, the answer depends on where in the country you look. While Scotland appears to provide a good example of multiparty competition in national and devolved elections, few other areas of the UK conform to this pattern. It is difficult to make a case for a three-party system, as the Liberal Democrats lack the national strength to compete with Labour and the Conservatives. The fickleness of the electorate only confuses the matter further. Not only has electoral volatility increased, but voters often choose different parties in different types of election, thus making it more difficult to identify any clear system.

It seems inappropriate at this stage to talk about the existence of a definite multiparty system in the UK. Ultimately, we may have to reconsider how to view party systems in the UK, and no longer look for a single form of party interaction. From an academic perspective, it may be more constructive to talk about a *variety* of party systems, each of which depends to a large extent on the mechanics of the electoral system in use and on where in the country you live.

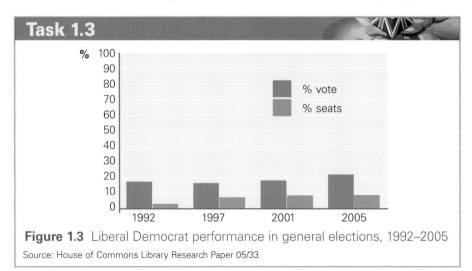

Task 1.3

Figure 1.3 Liberal Democrat performance in general elections, 1992–2005

Source: House of Commons Library Research Paper 05/33

Task 1.3 (continued)

Using Figure 1.3 and your own knowledge, argue the case that the performance of the Liberal Democrats in 2005 was worse than expected.

Guidance

Even though it has increased its representation in the House of Commons, in 13 years, the party has only managed to creep up a few percentage points. Its parliamentary increases arise largely out of a sophisticated seat-targeting strategy. The political situation in 2005 looked extremely favourable for the Liberal Democrats: a popular leader; a government under pressure for failing to deliver on public services and bogged down in two unpopular foreign wars; and a Conservative Party that was struggling to reach beyond its core electoral base. Even some prominent Liberal Democrats, such as Simon Hughes, expected the Liberal Democrats to break the 100-seat barrier in 2005.

Useful websites

- House of Commons Library paper on the 2005 general election
  www.parliament.uk/commons/lib/research/rp2005/rp05-033.pdf
- Pippa Norris on party systems
  http://ksghome.harvard.edu/~pnorris/ACROBAT/Institutions/Chapter%204.pdf

Further reading

- Fisher, J. (2003) 'All change? Party systems in Britain', *Politics Review*, Vol. 3, No. 1.
- Heffernan, R. (2005) 'Political parties and the party system', *Developments in British Politics 7*, Macmillan.

Is this the era of post-ideological parties?

For people whose main political education took place in the 1980s, against the backdrop of industrial unrest, mass marches against unemployment, the introduction of privatisation, ideas were what made politics fascinating. Of course, the major political figures of the age were worthy of attention themselves, but it was the ideas that influenced them which grabbed our attention. In hindsight, there was a certain pantomime element to the era, with few areas of grey or compromise. The first section in this chapter outlines the major ideas that influenced the main parties for most of the last century.

Patrick Chauvel/Sygma/Corbis

The Yorkshire Coal Strike, 1984

The twenty-first century, however, has been much less colourful in political terms. Turnout in elections is down; party elites see rigid, central control as a necessary prerequisite of electoral success; and there appears to be little difference in the policies on offer from the major parties. This chapter examines the view articulated by many respected political commentators that ideas no longer shape party policy programmes, and, as a consequence, there is little to choose between the parties on most major issues, beyond which party will be the most competent at managing the government of the country.

Put simply, are we living in an age in which ideas *do not matter*?

Main ideological traditions

The Conservatives

The first problem with outlining the main ideological traditions of the Conservative Party is that many would argue that it is pragmatism, rather than ideas, which forms the basis of Conservative attitudes. Viewed cynically, this could be interpreted merely as a desire to be in power. However, the pragmatism at the heart of Conservative thought is itself underpinned by certain beliefs and traditions. These include a negative view of human nature and a belief in hierarchy, defence of property, paternalism, emphasis on tradition, and the nation.

The second problem in identifying strands in modern Conservatism is that its post-1975 version apparently rejects several of these central tenets of traditional Conservatism. What may be useful to a student of Conservative ideas therefore is to provide a comparison of the different eras of Conservatism, in order to determine how consistent they have been (Table 2.1). The traditional version of Conservatism can be taken to represent the evolution of Conservative ideas from the start of the nineteenth century to the start of the 1970s. The modern version is that articulated by senior party leaders since Margaret Thatcher became leader of the party in 1975.

Table 2.1 'Traditional' and 'modern' Conservative ideas

Principle of Conservatism	Traditional Conservatism	Modern Conservatism	
		How it disagrees with traditional Conservatism	How it agrees with traditional Conservatism
(1) Reason and tradition	• Has a faith in values, customs and institutions that have stood the test of time, i.e. they are guided by 'what has worked'. • These would provide a sense of belonging, or identity, which would foster greater social cohesion. • Hence, supports common institutions such as the monarchy, House of Lords, Church of	• Policy influenced to a greater extent by political doctrine. Influential authors included Friedrich Hayek, and Milton Friedman. • Believes in the need for radical change.	

(2) Negative belief in human nature	• Humans are essentially anti-social, and therefore take comfort in social order. • Humans are believed to be morally flawed, greedy and hungry for power. • Human beings' intellectual powers are limited, which prevents them from introducing reforms that will improve on centuries of experience.	• To a large extent, based on (liberal) *theoretical* works advocating free-market economics.	• Attributes causes of crime to defects in human character.
(3) Hierarchical society	• Believes that all people are not born equal, and that a natural process of selection occurs. • Authority comes from above. Narrow view of democracy — voters give their consent to their rulers, but do not have the right to question their judgement. • All benefit from social inequality, as everyone has a stake in a stable, ordered society. • However, with greater authority comes a responsibility for the poor.	• Thatcher proclaimed that there was no such thing as society, simply a collection of individuals and their families. • Firm belief in meritocracy.	• Ensured that unelected union leaders were not able to hold the government to ransom.
(4) Defence of property	• Property rights were seen as part of the traditional social arrangements. • Inheritance of land ensured that property and values were passed on through the generations, thus maintaining the natural order of things. • Property owners would not be likely to support radical social change, which might undermine their place in society. • Property owners have a stake in society and are less likely to commit anti-social acts against other members of that society.		• Extension of home and share ownership necessary to ensure responsible behaviour and rejection of socialism.

(5) The nation and empire	• Conservatives claimed to stand above narrow sectional interests and represent the nation as a whole. • Support for the Union and the Empire were distinctly British and Conservative values.	• Defence of the Falklands against Argentinian invasion in 1982 demonstrated continued belief in a 'greater' Britain. • Defensive approach to European matters illustrates desire to maintain sovereignty of the British state.

Labour

For much of its history, the Labour Party has attempted to soften the harsher elements of capitalism and to offer a viable vision of a fairer society, albeit one that maintains capitalism as its dominant economic system. Although often associated with socialist ideology, Labour has traditionally offered a version of socialism called *social democracy,* as distinct from its ideological 'purer' alternative, *democratic socialism*.

Social democracy

Social democracy seeks to reform but not replace capitalism. This might be done by redistributing wealth through progressive taxation or the welfare state.

Democratic socialism

Like social democracy, democratic socialism is concerned with tackling the inequalities which capitalism creates. The key difference is in its strategy. It does not believe that capitalism is capable of reform, so democratic socialists seek to transform the structure of society.

Heywood (2003) identifies the following as the main features of social democracy, and by implication, Labour ideology, since the party's formation in 1906:
- a belief in parliamentary action rather than revolutionary socialism
- acceptance that capitalism is the most effective system for generating wealth
- unfettered capitalism inevitably creates poverty and inequality so it is 'morally defective'

The state, as guardian of the public interest, is a central instrument in rectifying the flaws inherent in capitalism. Clause IV of the 1918 party constitution committed Labour to securing 'common ownership of the means of production and control of each industry and service'. The main influences on Labour ideology are outlined in Figure 2.1.

Ethical socialism
Emphasised distinctive moral values, which soulless capitalism threatened.

Fabianism
Advocated a gradual transition to a socialist society. Believed that the state should play a prominent role in regulating people's lives.

Marxism
Critique of capitalism, and focus on the idea of class war sporadically influential, but largely at odds with dominant gradualist tendencies in the party.

Influences on Labour ideology

Trade unionism
Trade unions needed a party to represent their interests and those of ëworkingmen' in parliament.

'New' liberalism
Believed that the state had a responsibility to ensure equality of opportunity.

Figure 2.1 Main influences on Labour ideology

In practice, there was always a certain fluidity to Labour's brand of social democracy. What we would refer to as 'Old' Labour was itself a contested notion. On the one hand, certain senior members of the party emphasised the need for political pragmatism. Herbert Morrison, for example, stated that socialism was 'what the Labour government does'. Another group of senior figures, including chancellor of the exchequer Sir Stafford Cripps, however, argued for a more theoretical approach to achieving the party's aims.

Even those who advocated underpinning Labour policy with a coherent set of ideas disagreed on the best ways to reform capitalism. In the 1950s a debate raged. Revisionists, such as Anthony Crosland, argued that Labour's post-war economic reforms had effectively tamed capitalism, so the party ought to focus on removing inequalities through progressive social measures, such as the introduction of comprehensive education. Crosland's most controversial proposal, in his book *The Future of Socialism* (1956), was that the party drop its commitment to state ownership and the planned economy.

The principal opponent of Crosland's ideas, Nye Bevan, disagreed with the view that capitalism had been reformed. Bevan claimed that it had barely been touched and the threat of widespread inequality remained. As a result, further nationalisation was required if the condition of Labour's natural constituency, the working class, was to be improved.

The debate about Labour's relationship to capitalism and the role of the state was to continue until well into the 1990s.

Liberal Democrats

The Liberal Democrats are technically the youngest of the major parties, being formed in 1988. Their roots, however, lie in the fusion of two existing parties: the Liberals and the Social Democratic Party. The SDP was formed in 1981 by disillusioned members of the Labour Party, who believed that the party had become distanced from its social democrat roots. It fought the 1983 and 1987 general elections in alliance with the Liberal Party. However, the fading support for the Liberal–SDP Alliance by the late 1980s led to a merger of the two parties, after a separate vote in each party. In many respects, the merger was inevitable given the overlap between the dominant ideas in each party. Each of these parties has contributed key elements to Liberal Democrat thought, but it is the Liberal Party that is the natural predecessor of the current Liberal Democrats (Figure 2.2).

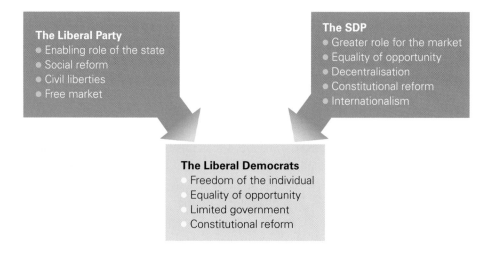

Figure 2.2 Evolution of the Liberal Democratic Party

Is there such a thing as the 'new politics'?

The term 'new politics' refers primarily to the lack of major disagreement between the major parties in the post-Thatcher age. While most commentators argue that a new consensus is based around the Thatcherite legacy of market-driven economic policy, and a reduced role for the state, a few suggest that 10 years of Labour government have moved the area of shared ideas leftwards.

The 'new' politics also refers to the different way in which political parties approach issues. Instead of approaching issues from an ideological perspective, as characterised by the 'old' politics, parties now value pragmatism rather than ideology.

Evidence for the existence of a new consensus

Perhaps, unsurprisingly, the Labour Party made the biggest contribution to the new consensus, rebranding itself as New Labour after the election of Tony Blair as party leader in 1994. Blair talked about creating a new politics, neither left nor right, following what has been termed a 'Third Way' between classical liberalism and democratic socialism. This led Blair to embark on an extensive overhaul of Labour's approaches to key areas of policy in the period 1994–97 (Figure 2.3).

Tony Blair

Abandoned Clause IV and its commitment to nationalisation.

Revised social policy, placed greater emphasis on individual responsibility.

Promised not to exceed Conservative spending limits for the first 2 years of a new administration and pledged not to raise income tax.

Figure 2.3　Labour ideology: old to new

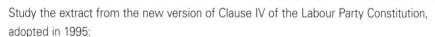

Task 2.1

Study the extract from the new version of Clause IV of the Labour Party Constitution, adopted in 1995:

> The Labour Party is a democratic socialist party. It believes that by the strength of our common endeavour we achieve more than we achieve alone, so as to create for each of us the means to realise our true potential and for all of us a community in which power, wealth and opportunity are in the hands of the many, not the few. Where the rights we enjoy reflect the duties we owe. And where we live together, freely, in a spirit of solidarity, tolerance and respect.

How does the new Clause IV suggest that the aims of New Labour differ from those of 'Old' Labour?

Task 2.1 (continued)

Guidance

Both the old and new versions accepted the existence of a capitalist economic system. Both aimed to lessen the effects of the harsher elements of this system on the working person and to allow each person to fulfil his/her potential. A sense of community, and belief in the existence of society, is a common theme as well.

Where they differ is in their attitude to equality. The old version implied equality in itself was a goal for the party, whereas the new version is concerned only with equality of opportunity, and this is counter-balanced with an awareness of the duties which each citizen has to the state. They also differ in the methods by which a person will achieve his/her goals. In the original version, this would be through common ownership of the means of production, whereas New Labour believes that it is mainly through hard work — *the strength of our common endeavour.*

Once in power, Labour arguably offered continuity rather than conflict with the approach of previous Conservative administrations. A study of Labour's approach in three key policy areas demonstrates this.

Economic policy

- Belief that the market can provide some services better than the state.
- Low inflation, rather than full employment, is the main economic priority.
- Supply-side economics, rather than Keynesian demand management, provides the most effective means of creating prosperity.
- High levels of taxation believed to prove a disincentive to individual effort.

Law and order

- Individuals need to take greater responsibility for their actions. The causes of crime are not purely environmental.
- Restrictions on individual liberties are a necessary price to pay in order to preserve the well-being of the majority.
- Prison works.
- The police need greater powers in order to reduce crime.

Health

- Emphasis on patient choice.
- Involvement of the private sector in constructing hospitals and reducing waiting times for treatment.

The Conservatives' response to successive Labour victories has arguably lacked ideological clarity and consistency. While it has attempted to outflank Labour on the right on issues such as immigration and Europe, it has settled on meeting Labour on the centre ground on issues such as public spending on health and education.

David Cameron's election as Conservative leader in 2005 does not look as though it will break the consensus. The values of Cameron's Conservative Party are outlined on the front cover of the policy document *Built to Last* (written in February 2006, revised in September 2006, and supported by 93% of those who participated in the internal party referendum (turnout was only 27% of total membership):

David Cameron

Our Party seeks to cherish freedom, advance opportunity and nurture responsibility. By trusting people, we help individuals grow stronger; by sharing responsibility, we help society grow stronger. We believe that there is such a thing as society, but it is not the same thing as the state. Our Party stands for a free society and a strong nation state; an opportunity society, not an overpowering state; a responsible society in which each person and every family, regardless of position or power or wealth, is able to fulfil their potential, to make their own choices, and to find true and lasting happiness.

The aims of the party include:
- Encouraging enterprise in all its forms — in the economy and in the community — in order to raise living standards and the quality of life for all.
- Fighting social injustice and helping the most disadvantaged by building a strong society.
- Meeting the great environmental threats of the age, to enhance the environment and to increase general well-being.
- Providing first-class healthcare, education and housing that respond to the needs of each individual. (This is not the same as the state trying to run our public services.)

Much of what Cameron says could be termed 'Blairite'. What could be pointed to in particular, are his acceptance of the existence of society (a significant departure from Thatcherism) and his emphasis on the need to develop individual potential (classic 'Third Wayism'). In an interview with the *New Statesman* in June 2006, Cameron even went so far as to advocate a more redistributive tax system.

Task 2.2

(a) Do the main aims of *Built to Last* suggest that the consensus is now built on a mixture of capitalism and social democracy?

(b) Is David Cameron a Conservative?

Guidance

(a) It certainly provides ample evidence of the emergence of a new consensus. The party's aims and the revised Labour Clause IV contain remarkably similar themes — opportunity, hard work, belief in society, sense of responsibility among citizens, tolerance.

(b) On the surface at least, the answer would appear to be 'no'. Cameron's approach since assuming the leadership seems to have been to make voters forget which party he belongs to: publicly calling for greater corporate responsibility; making statements on global warming; criticising the UK's relationship with the USA; hugging hoodies? Even so, given his background in public relations, and the party's disastrous performances in 1997–2005, Cameron's priority since 2005 was always going to be changing the way people think about the Conservative Party — hence, his subtle rebranding of the party's image. In terms of policy baggage, he has certainly 'travelled light', but his work in the party before his election may prove enlightening. He was, after all, the man regarded as chiefly responsible for writing the 2005 manifesto, which was one of the most economically liberal and socially conservative documents the party has ever produced.

A study of the policy positions of each of the three main parties during the 2005 general election demonstrates further the extent to which a new consensus exists (Table 2.2).

Table 2.2 Party policy positions, 2005 general election

Policy area	Labour	Conservative	Liberal Democrat
Tax and the economy	• Low inflation the prime economic goal. • No increase in basic or higher rates of income tax. • Raise stamp duty threshold. • Small increase in public spending.	• Low inflation the prime economic goal. • Plan tax cuts. • Aim to relieve burden of stamp duty on properties over £250,000. • Small increase in public spending.	• Low inflation the prime economic goal. • New 50% top rate of income tax on £100,000+. • Raise stamp duty threshold.

Law and order	• Maintain record levels of police numbers. • More prison places. • Increased resources for drug treatment.	• Recruit extra police. • More prison places. • Increased resources for drug treatment. • Tougher enforcement of ASBOs.	• Recruit extra police. • Fewer ASBOs. • Decriminalise personal cannabis use.
Health	• Extend patient choice of hospital. • Use private sector to help reduce waiting times. • Action on MRSA.	• Extend patient choice of hospital. • State to pay 50% of the cost for private operations. • Action on MRSA.	• Reduce diagnostic waiting times. • More prescriptions. • Free long-term care for the elderly.
Education	• Greater independence for schools. • Establish new specialist schools. • Limited selection on aptitude. • More powers to tackle disruptive behaviour. • University 'top-up' fees.	• Greater independence for schools. • Allow creation of more grammar schools. • More powers to tackle disruptive behaviour. • Charge graduates interest on student loans.	• Remove a number of tests. • Scrap university tuition fees.

However, to argue for the existence of a new politics merely on the basis of a new consensus would be weak. We also have to consider the *removal of ideology* from party politics.

Critics of the Third Way claim that it lacks a strong ideological core and appears to represent a collection of disconnected values rather than a prescription for a new society. Its lack of depth thus enables its followers to interpret it as their needs dictate.

Furthermore, Labour's critics suggest that policy is influenced chiefly by electoral considerations, i.e. a desire to avoid alienating as many voters as possible, and it has therefore followed the mood of the country rather than attempting to set the agenda. Inevitably, this has resulted in a package of measures that lacks consistency or coherence. On the one hand, the chancellor introduces a windfall tax on the privatised utilities and, on the other, states that, if necessary, public spending would be cut before taxes were increased.

Chapter 2

Challenges to a new politics

New Labour is merely 'Old' Labour adapted to the global market

- The party maintains a commitment to equality of opportunity.
- It has always accepted the role of a mixed economy, with state intervention seen as a means rather than an end in itself.
- Only the changed economic context since the mid-1970s has forced Labour to achieve its aims in different ways.

Major issues still divide the parties

- **Constitutional reform**. The Conservatives reject any attempt to reform the electoral system or to introduce regional assemblies and Labour's plans to reform the House of Lords.
- **Europe**. Labour was prepared to support the European Constitution, which the Conservatives opposed. Gordon Brown established five tests for possible UK membership of the euro, which Conservatives have rejected out of hand.
- **Tax**. In 2005, the Conservatives promised to introduce tax cuts worth £4bn, while Labour has no intention of doing so.
- **Equality**. Bobbio (1996) argues that this is the fundamental difference between the parties. He matches Labour's commitment to reduce inequality with proclamations such as that by David Willets in 1992, when he stated that equality was the *key anti-Conservative concept*. In David Cameron's interview with the *New Statesman*, referred to on page 33, he actually argues for a redistributive tax system, yet states that the inequality which exists between the extremely wealthy and those on benefits is not of 'greatest concern'. Fielding (1999) claims that equality is Labour's *distinct, if ultimate aim*, and is the biggest area of disagreement with previous Conservative governments. Even in opposition, the Conservatives opposed a series of Labour measures, such as the windfall tax and the introduction of a minimum wage, whose intention was to reduce inequality.

Disagreement over what the consensus is based on

Left-of-centre commentators argue that Blairism is Conservatism with a human face — Labour having accepted the victory of free-market capitalism and dropped its commitment to state intervention in the economy. However, as Fairclough et al. (2006) point out, some right-leaning newspapers believe that the Conservatives have moved to the left as a result of Labour's recent electoral dominance. The point is this: if people cannot agree on what the parties are supposed to agree on, how can a consensus exist at all?

Consensus was the norm in post-war British politics

Britain's political parties have agreed on most major areas of policy since 1945. The Conservatives responded to their defeat in 1945 by accepting the existence of the welfare state and NHS, with prominent government intervention in the economy. Even during the Thatcher years the Conservatives left the main aspects of the post-war settlement in place. The NHS remained free at the point of access; the welfare state, although undermined, still served to provide a safety net for the most vulnerable in society; and privatisation had clear limits. For example, the railways, the National Coal Board, and Air Traffic Control were all privatised after Thatcher left office, and Air Traffic Control was privatised by a Labour government. Labour's trimming of the state has continued into its third term. In March 2006, Gordon Brown announced plans to sell off the state-owned nuclear industry, the Tote, public spectrum airwaves and Ministry of Defence firing ranges.

Both parties have traditionally favoured pragmatism over ideology

The 'winner takes all' nature of Britain's electoral system ensures that no party wishing to form a government can afford to alienate large sections of the electorate. Both Labour and Conservative parties have thus been pushed towards the centre of the political spectrum. Above all, circumstance and electoral necessity have played a bigger role in determining policy positions than abstract doctrine. Two critical elections, 1945 and 1979, illustrate this point perfectly. Both elections are often seen as marking a turning point in the nature of the dominant political ideology. In the first instance, the election heralded the arrival of statist social democracy, and in the second case it marked the end of the social democratic consensus and its replacement by *laissez-faire* free-market ideas.

However, it could be argued that Labour's post-war programme in 1945 was heavily influenced by several non-socialist factors:

(1) Several industries were clearly failing in private ownership before the Second World War.

(2) The experience of a planned economy had proved to be a success during the war.

(3) Labour activists were actually told to play down plans for nationalisation, for fear of alienating middle-class voters.

(4) The welfare state and the use of demand management to stimulate the economy were the ideas of liberals (e.g. William Beveridge and John Maynard Keynes), not socialists.

Equally, non-ideological factors had an impact upon Conservative policies after 1979:

(1) Labour had dropped demand management in 1976, in response to rising inflation and rising unemployment.

(2) The Conservatives successfully tapped into areas where levels of popular discontent were high: union power, rising inflation, taxation.

Why has a new consensus emerged?

The impact of globalisation

The ability of governments to set their own economic goals has been limited by the growing power of financial speculators, who, exploiting advances in technology and the abolition of exchange controls, are able to pulverise a currency overnight. The principal effect on governments has been to force on them policies that encourage low inflation, rather than tackle unemployment. Low inflation implies economic stability, low costs, and above all, a stable currency.

With the emergence of global labour, employers have proved willing to relocate to countries where labour costs and labour flexibility are lower. This has meant that governments have been pressured to keep taxes low, and limit wage increases. In practical terms, this has spelt the end of union power and Keynesian 'tax and spend' Labour fiscal policy.

Increasing levels of international trade have ensured that UK firms must be competitive if they are to be successful both in resisting the threat from imports and in selling their goods on the international market. This has added further pressure to keep labour costs and levels of taxation down:

> …to make Britain's economy more competitive, to promote innovation and to remove barriers to business and wealth creation. Foremost in our minds are the commercial interests of UK plc.
>
> Stated aims of the Conservative policy group on competitiveness, 2005
> www.competitivechallenge.com/

> In a fast changing global economy, government cannot postpone or prevent change. The modern role for government — the case for a modern employment and skills policy — is to equip people to succeed, to be on their side, helping them become more skilled, adaptable and flexible for the job ahead.
>
> *Britain Forward Not Back*, Labour Party Manifesto, 2005

Playing to the gallery

Declining voter turnout has also played its part in moving the parties closer together. Adapting rational choice theory, parties will seek to maximise their popularity among those groups who are most likely to vote. The bulk of their policies will therefore be constructed with these voters in mind. A study of turnout in elections since the end of the 1970s highlights the decline in the number of people prepared to vote, with the most reluctant voters to be found among the unemployed and manual sector (Table 2.3 and Figure 2.4).

| Table 2.3 | Illustration of falling turnout in inner city constituencies |

Lowest turnout in 1997	%
Liverpool Riverside	51.6
Manchester Central	51.7
Hackney North and Stoke Newington	52.0
Sheffield Central	53.0
Leeds Central	54.2

Each seat held by a Labour MP.

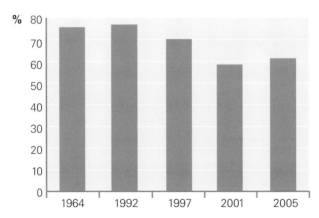

Figure 2.4 Turnout in recent elections (1964 included as an example of turnout during the era of alignment)

Source: 'A strong case of election apathy' (http://news.bbc.co.uk)

The impact on party programmes is profound. No party has a vested interest in prioritising issues that exclusively affect poorer members of the electorate. Similarly, as each party's room for manoeuvre with policy is limited, greater emphasis is placed on reacting to what voters want, via focus groups and greater public consultation. This contributes further to the de-ideologisation of British politics; and the arrival of 'Paul Weller politics' (to quote his first band, The Jam, 'what the public wants, the public gets'). This has resulted in the continued pursuit of a tight fiscal policy, with no increase in income tax, and limited public spending, and an emphasis on maintaining low inflation.

The decline of class voting

The significance of class-based voting in establishing a stable party system is documented on page 9, but the rightwards movement of Labour under Neil Kinnock and Tony Blair, and the Conservatives' reluctance to put too much ideological water between themselves and Labour, can, to a certain extent, be explained by two conflicting theories concerning class and voting behaviour.

Theory 1: the shrinking working class

Heath et al. argue that while Labour's share of the vote among its natural supporters has changed little since 1979, the actual size of this group has shrunk, thus providing an explanation for Labour's declining share of the vote since then.

Exacerbating the impact of the shrinking working class, the evolution of a more ethnically diverse society meant that people did not identify in class terms in the same way as they had done in the immediate post-war era. With the certainty of a strong core vote under threat, Labour had to adapt or wither away.

In response to this, Labour was forced to transform itself from being a mass party to a catch-all party, thereby removing any accusation that it remained a sectional party, i.e. one that represented only the unions and working class. Hence its abolition of the old Clause IV, and further commitments designed to remove any images of 'Old' Labour governments.

Theory 2: the class dealignment thesis

The nature of this theory has been outlined in detail elsewhere (see Smith 2006), but essentially it argues that class is no longer a key determinant in voting behaviour.

This is because class dealignment has contributed to the convergence of party positions in two ways. First, Labour tried to effect class *realignment* by emphasising its commitment to key public services and by embracing the more populist elements of Conservative criminal justice policy. Second, both parties have converged on the centre ground and made their appeal to the electorate largely on the basis of managerial competence. A recent example of this was provided by the Conservatives' announcement in August 2006 that they had created a 'delivery watchdog' to monitor government promises and study how many are not followed through. Their main purpose is to establish the message that Labour is not necessarily flawed in its approach, but less efficient in its delivery of policies than the Conservatives would be.

Electoral necessity

This reason overlaps with several of those previously explained. Put simply, parties that repeatedly lose elections have to adapt their message if they are to win power again. It assumes that losing parties attempt to ape key aspects of successful parties' platforms in order to maximise their chances of taking office after future elections.

From Labour's perspective, losing four elections in a row proved difficult to accept. Indeed, some in the party questioned whether Labour could ever win power, particularly as the Major government had prevailed at a time of economic uncertainty. Although Neil Kinnock had initiated a modernisation programme after the 1987 defeat, members of the party believed that he had not gone far enough. In a 1992 pamphlet for the Fabian Society entitled *Southern Discomfort*, Giles Radice argued that Labour had lost touch with upwardly mobile voters who had once supported the party, and had to do more to attract voters, particularly those in the south and southeast. After he became leader in 1994, Tony Blair demonstrated some sympathy with Radice's ideas, feeling that Labour had committed a major error in ignoring what many voters wanted during previous decades. While voters wanted to enjoy the fruits of their labours, the party had continued to endorse the growth of a powerful and expensive state, something which would be serviced by higher rates of taxation. As a result, the party had suffered badly in the polling booth.

Blair's response was to incorporate greater acceptance of individualism into his brand of social democracy and to downplay the importance of the state in managing the economy and wealth creation.

Since 1997, the Conservatives have found themselves in a similar, though not as extreme, position as Labour did at the start of the decade. Having lived through a century during which the Conservative Party was in power for over 70% of the time, they faced the prospect of having to endure an era of prolonged Labour dominance. After the 2005 general election, the party still has fewer than 200 MPs — fewer than Labour's lowest total in all its 18 years of opposition. Moreover, the Conservatives faced their own form of 'northern discomfort', finding it impossible to win seats in any major cities outside London. In order to regain power, they have to shake off the perception that they are a narrowly based sectional party. Perhaps it is the need to revive their ability to appeal

beyond their core base which has led them to adopt significant elements of Labour's agenda. These include acceptance of the minimum wage, the Working Families Tax Credit and a greater emphasis on dealing with global issues such as climate change (Box 2.1).

Box 2.1

Why did the Conservatives fail to appeal to a broad electorate?

The party's failure to go far enough to appeal to a broader base of supporters was high-lighted by former minister Tim Yeo shortly after the 2005 general election:

> Our task is to show not only that we share these concerns but that we have better answers. A greater willingness to tackle some non-traditional issues would help too. Conservatives are naturally environmentalists, so it's high time we put the environment at the heart of our agenda. There's widespread agreement that climate change is one of the main problems facing the world; and it is something on which Tony Blair is particularly vulnerable as his approach so far has been all talk and no action.

> Before the election I worked up a proposal for huge tax cuts to encourage the purchase and use of the greenest, cleanest cars, to be paid for by higher levies on the gas guzzlers, but found it blocked by nervousness that the owners of Chelsea tractors would somehow be the group that denied us victory at the polls. But it is precisely in areas like this that we can prove we are able to confront the most urgent challenges of the 21st century.

> Tim Yeo (2005) 'Rightwards is not a route to power', *Guardian*, 10 May

---

What are the consequences of the 'new politics'?

Falling levels of turnout

As Figure 2.4 illustrated, turnout at the last two general elections has reached its lowest levels yet. Turnout for most general elections has rarely topped 80% anyway, but we appear to be living in an age of widespread disengagement with the formal political process. For example in 2005, for the first time in history, those voting for the winning party were outnumbered by those who did not vote. Speaking in 2003, Robin Cook described voters as 'spectators of political theatre'. Several sources suggest that the lack of real choice between the parties, and the removal of ideas from political competition have contributed significantly to this development.

Established in 2004 by The Joseph Rowntree Trust, the Power Inquiry spent 18 months talking to voters about why they are so disengaged from politics. It discovered that declining turnout in elections contrasted sharply with evidence suggesting that interest in politics was high. Three of its explanations for low turnout focus on the role of ideology in shaping the policies of British political parties. First, the inquiry claimed that *the main political parties are widely perceived to be too similar*, second that they are *lacking in principle*; and third that political *parties and elections require citizens to commit to too broad a range of policies*.

These explanations relate directly to the effects of the 'new politics'. Voters, it seems, want a choice between two competing programmes; without one, there appears little incentive to replace one set of politicians with another. However, turnout was not such a problem during the period of the 'old' post-war consensus, so why is the advent of a new consensus a factor in low turnout? The second and third explanations provide the clue. They suggest that voters do not see politics as simple management and delivery; it is about a much wider purpose. If this was not the case, why do more people get involved in non-party political activity than ever before? The third explanation is interesting because it implies that a worrying consequence of both parties transforming themselves into 'catch-all' parties has been to lose the distinctiveness which drove people to support them in the first place.

> The catch-all strategy, appealing to a broader but more thinly distributed range of individuals, may lose the electoral bonus that social interaction can bring.
> Heath, Curtice and Jowell (2001) *The Rise of New Labour: Party Policies and Voter Choices*

Decline in support for the main parties

The extent to which the main parties have lost electoral support as a result of the new consensus is open to debate. However, evidence to support the proposition is not hard to find:

- Labour and Conservative joint share of the vote has fallen since the mid-1950s; the figure for 2005 was almost 30% lower than in 1951. The year 2005 was also the first time that their share of the vote had fallen below 70% since the Second World War.
- Voters who would be expected to regularly turn out for either the Labour or Conservative parties have provided crucial support for rival, smaller parties on occasion. In 1997, the Conservatives leaked a small but significant number of voters to the Referendum Party, and have done so at European and regional level to UKIP. This trend has continued in recent by-elections, with UKIP beating the Conservatives into fourth place in Hartlepool in 2005 and third place, ahead of Labour, in Bromley and Chislehurst in 2006.

The main fear of those members of the Labour Party who were sceptical about the crusade for the middle-class vote was that the party would leave working-class voters with nowhere to go but the political extremes. As Figure 2.5 indicates, the evidence so far would suggest that these fears have been partially realised.

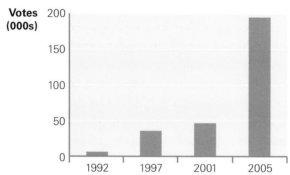

Figure 2.5 Growth in support for the British National Party in general elections, 1992–2005

Source: House of Commons Library Research Paper 05/33

Although the BNP was not successful in the 2005 general election, it enjoyed its best campaign to date. In addition to increasing its total vote substantially, it achieved partial successes in a small number of Labour-held constituencies, gaining 17% of the vote in Barking (beating the Liberal Democrats into fourth place). The BNP also gained 9.2% of the vote in Keighley, where party chair Nick Griffin was standing, and 13.1% in Dewsbury. It performed even better in the 2006 local council elections, managing to double the party's number of council seats. The party made it clear after the results that its success was based on disillusionment with the two main parties, but especially with the Labour Party (see Box 2.2).

Box 2.2

Explaining the BNP's success?

[The party's success was due to] people wanting to kick the Labour Party really hard and we're the politically incorrect way to do it. When you look at some of our results elsewhere in the country where we've hammered the Conservatives as well, this is a revolt against the entire liberal political elite by the hardworking people of Britain who resent being taxed to have our country transformed.

Nick Griffin, leader of the BNP

This is Labour's third term and they've done nothing for the country. People are sick and tired of all the lies. We are offering people a choice.

Solihull BNP councillor, George Morgan

- The main beneficiaries from disillusionment with the main parties have been the Liberal Democrats, who have, through skilful campaigning, proved capable of taking seats from both parties. Their performance in 2005 also saw them achieve the highest share of the vote by a third party since the 23.1% gained by the SDP–Liberal Alliance in 1983.
- Decline in support for the major parties can also be measured through a study of falling party memberships. Between 1997 and 2005, Labour membership more than halved, falling from 410,000 to 201,374 (the party had 840,000 members in the mid-1960s). The Conservatives experienced a similar drop; falling from 400,000 in 1997 to 253,600 in 2005. During the course of its inquiry into political participation, the Power Commission (2004–06) found that the most common reason for not joining or leaving a political party was the *move away from competing ideologies to consensus, managerialism or opportunism.* In his submission to the inquiry, Francis Maude MP, Conservative co-chairperson, stated that:

> I think people don't feel so passionately about party politics as they did. They think conventional party politics matters less than it did and they're right that it does: the gulf between the parties is less than it was. In conventional sort of left/right terms the range of the compass that is covered by the political parties is less than it was so people feel less threatened by the alternatives. They don't feel it makes as much difference. A change of government today makes less difference than it did 20 years ago.

Learning point

Is Francis Maude right to claim that a change of government today makes less difference than it did 20 years ago?

Evidence of large-scale defections to minor parties not wholly conclusive
- Support for the main parties at general elections has remained at around 70% since 1974.
- Labour has not lost masses of voters to more socialist parties that might have expected to benefit from the party's move to the right. The Socialist Labour Party polled 52,000 votes in 1997, yet this figure fell to 20,000 in 2005, and they lost all but one of their deposits in the 49 constituencies where they fielded candidates. In Scotland, the performance of the Scottish Socialist Party was remarkably similar, falling from 72,000 votes in 2001 to 43,000 in 2005, losing all but two out of 58 deposits. Even the effects of PR did not enable the SSP to make an impact, finishing as the sixth largest party, with fewer MSPs than the Greens. Although it is too soon to assess the fall-out from the libel case won by its former leader, Tommy Sheridan, the only certainty is that the Scottish socialist vote will be even more divided at the next election.

New forms of political engagement

Even though the number of people participating in formal party politics has decreased, this does not mean that the number of people acting politically has also fallen. Instead, as Gerry Stoker (2006) points out, citizens are increasingly getting involved in local and single-issue campaigns. Using data provided by the European Social Survey (see Figure 2.6), he has shown that the *pattern* of political activity in the UK has changed considerably since the 1980s. Whereas people used to be more likely to engage in a *collective* type of political activity, such as joining a party or pressure group, activity in the twenty-first century tends to be on a more individual and micro level.

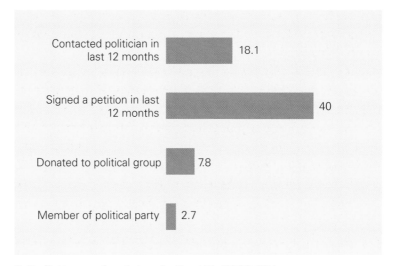

Figure 2.6 Patterns of activism in the UK, 2002 (%)

Source: G. Stoker (2006) *Why Politics Matters: Making Democracy Work*

The Council of Europe report, *The Future of Democracy in Europe* (2004), presented several reasons for growing disengagement with formal politics and the changing nature of political activity, but gave one reason in particular which is relevant to the development of the 'new politics' — a belief that ideas and principles no longer mattered to the parties. As there was no real difference between the parties, there was thus little incentive to vote for or join a party.

Learning point

Should we be concerned by changing patterns of activism?

Conclusion

The submissions made to the Power Inquiry appear to suggest that a broad consensus of opinion exists on this issue, irrespective of political background. Those on the right such as Francis Maude and Alan Duncan agree with old Labourites such as Michael Meacher that ideology has disappeared from British politics and the effects are unwelcome. The problem with this perspective is that it has all been said before. Every student of A-level politics is given at least an overview of British politics between 1945 and 1979, and is taught that a consensus between the parties held for most of this period. A few students might even be directed towards Daniel Bell's work *The End of Ideology*, which was published in 1960. Bell's thesis was that the existing ideologies of socialism and conservatism were no longer relevant in the middle of the twentieth century, as capitalism had in effect been tamed.

Yet, on reflection, references to the post-war consensus glossed over major areas of disagreement between the major parties. The Conservatives, for example, resisted any further nationalisation, whereas Labour argued for further control by the state. The same point should be made regarding the new politics in the modern era. Yes, there are agreements on how the economic and criminal justice systems should be run, but there are major differences of principle and policy. Crucially, Labour still believes that the state has a positive role to play in the management of the economy, particularly in helping out the least fortunate in society. The minimum wage, the New Deal and the Working Families Tax Credit are good examples of the state actively intervening to improve the quality of life for its citizens. Each of these measures was opposed by the Conservatives.

Task 2.3

How has the emergence of a new consensus contributed to falling voter turnout?

Guidance
It has had an impact in two ways. First, rational choice theorists would argue that the emergence of a new consensus gives the impression that all parties are the same and that voting is therefore unlikely to make any difference. Second, the new consensus may dissuade people from participating in conventional political activity as the parties adopt vote-maximising strategies at the expense of ideology; people may choose instead to join a pressure group or participate in local campaigns.

Useful websites

- Liberal History Group
  www.liberalhistory.org.uk/
- The Power Inquiry and Report
  www.powerinquiry.org/
- The Future of Democracy in Europe
  www.coe.int/t/e/integrated_projects/democracy/05_key_texts/02_Green_Paper/index.asp#
  TopOfPage

Further reading

- Fielding, S. (2000) 'A new politics?', in P. Dunleavy, A. Gamble, I. Holliday and G. Peele (eds) *Developments in British Politics*, Macmillan, pp. 10–28.
- Leach, R. (2002) *Political Ideology in Britain*, Palgrave Macmillan, pp. 226–34.
- Smith, N. (2006) *UK Elections & Electoral Reform*, Philip Allan Updates.

Do parties promote democracy?

Much of what has been written about public attitudes towards political parties suggests that they are thought to be self-serving, unprincipled and occasionally corrupt. As was suggested in Chapter 2, many people participate in some form of political activity in the UK which does not involve any of the political parties.

Such scepticism is not new. Writing in 1938, Harold Laski acknowledged that parties:

> …distort the issues that they create. They produce divisions in the electorate which very superficially represent the way in which opinion is in fact distributed…They falsify the perspective of the issues they create.

However, Laski's intention was actually to defend the role parties play in modern democracies:

> Yet when the last criticisms of party have been made the services they render to a democratic state are inestimable.

This chapter examines how relevant political parties are to the democratic process in the twenty-first century, and whether the contributions they make to democracy in the UK are as valuable as Laski argued in the late 1930s.

Do political parties perform a useful function in modern democracies?

The role of political parties differs considerably according to the type of political regime they are based in and on particular circumstances within states sharing similar political systems.

In a one-party system, the role of the party may, to a large extent, be concerned with the preservation of power; be it as a front for a personality-based regime or possibly as the principal source of coercion. Clearly, parties in liberal democracies perform a greater range of roles, but these too may differ depending on the consequences of different electoral systems, the nature of party systems or

even the extent of public support for parties within that system. The following analysis outlines six main functions of political parties in liberal democracies, with a discussion of how far parties are still capable of performing these roles.

Integration and mobilisation

In the era before universal suffrage, parties (or factions as they are more likely to have been) had no need to mobilise the electorate. Usually patronage or tradition would be sufficient to direct someone's vote. However, the introduction of mass suffrage during the nineteenth century meant that parties had to perform two new functions:(i) integrating new ideas into their manifesto, and (ii) mobilising the electorate to vote for their candidates. By taking into account the desires and ideas of the people, parties can claim to truly represent the interests of their voters. Persuading the electorate to vote for their policies enables the winning party to claim a mandate for those policies.

This is arguably the most important function which parties have to perform. When the main parties fail to integrate new ideas into their programme, and effectively lose touch with the electorate, or fail to effectively get out the vote, then the party system as a whole will most likely be threatened. It is for this reason that issues such as dealignment, declining party membership and the fall in voter turnout are attracting the attention of both academics and political leaders.

Organising political competition

In most liberal democracies, parties have historically acted as a device to allow people to be elected. Indeed, political success is usually dependent on a party label. Even where party ties are relatively weak, as in the USA for example, candidates still rely on attachment to a party in order to enhance their chance of election to the legislature. At election times, choice between candidates in most liberal democratic countries has little to do with individual personalities, although different electoral systems, for example the Open List or Single Transferable Vote systems, can moderate the domination of party. The ways in which parties perform this role are varied and are illustrated in Figure 3.1.

Figure 3.1 Ways in which parties organise political competition

Parties continue to perform this role once the election is over and MPs are in the House of Commons. The principal function of a non-government party in the legislature is to hold the government to account, by scheduling debates, submitting written and oral questions, participating on parliamentary committees and instructing its MPs on when and how to vote. The parties are also able to put aside political differences to make administrative agreements between themselves. For example, the practice of pairing describes the situation when an MP from one party cannot attend a vote in the Commons, and a *pair* from a rival party agrees not to vote as well. In this way, parties do not suffer when one of their MPs is ill, or has a genuine reason not to vote. Parties also cooperate in the organisation of business in the Commons. Each week, the government chief whip will provide his/her opposition counterpart with details of the government's business programme, and no final decision is taken by the government until after consultation with him/her.

Parties may sometimes introduce measures to preserve their role as sole organisers of political competition. After a number of Conservative back-benchers rebelled over the issue of the government's signing of the Maastricht Treaty, the party decided to remove the whip from the dissident MPs. In the run-up to the 2005 election, leader Michael Howard removed the whip from deputy chair Howard Flight and barred him from standing again as a Conservative candidate after he suggested that Conservative plans to cut red tape would be more extensive than had been outlined by the leadership. In 1997, Labour introduced a Code of Conduct which all of its MPs had to sign. It stated that 'no member of the Parliamentary Labour Party shall engage in a sustained course of conduct prejudicial to the party'. In this way, the party hoped to maintain the loyalty of its MPs. In the Scottish Parliament, Conservative MSP Brian Monteith had the whip removed in 2005 for briefing against the former leader of the party.

However, the importance of parties in organising political competition can vary between political systems. In states where a proportional system of election is used, the diverse nature of the assembly can lead to the creation of alliances between factions from different parties. Temporary alliances can sometimes occur if majoritarian systems are used as well. Both Conservative and Labour administrations have experienced significant rebellions by backbench MPs on crucial House of Commons votes. Since the 2005 general election, 80 Labour and 29 Conservative backbench MPs have revolted against the party whip.

However, punishing rebel backbenchers for disloyalty does not guarantee that the authority of the party will be automatically restored. After the nine Tory rebels were readmitted to the party, they behaved in a way which suggested that

they, rather than their party, were more important. In his memoirs, former prime minister John Major is highly critical of their conduct after their return from 'exile'. He writes, 'they held a cocky, unapologetic press conference…They made no conciliatory noises, and refused to give any guarantees of party loyalty'. It is also worth noting here that, in spite of the code of conduct, no Labour MP has had the whip withdrawn for the way that he/she has voted since 1997.

MPs may also lose their party loyalties when acting as a member of a select committee. The select committee system was established in 1980, with the aim of improving scrutiny of the work of the main government departments. The committees take evidence from ministers, civil servants and other relevant experts and report to the House of Commons on their conclusions.

John Major

Many MPs also join all-party groups which have a specific interest in either a certain topic or country. These groups are a more informal source of influence than select committees and act as a form of lobby group within the legislature.

Recruitment of political personnel

Parties recruit political personnel on several levels.

To the government

In parliamentary systems, political parties enjoy a virtual monopoly of recruitment of personnel to the executive. Every member of the current Labour government is a member of the Labour Party and either an MP or member of the House of Lords. The prime minister is leader of the leading party, following a long-established convention that the leader of the largest party in the House of Commons is invited to form a government by the monarch. John Prescott was appointed deputy prime minister by Tony Blair simply because he was deputy leader of the Labour Party.

However, members of the government may also be drawn from a wider pool of talent. This is most notably the case in presidential systems, notably the USA, but Tony Blair has not been afraid to appoint people from outside the party ranks. His first ministerial appointments included the former chair of British Petroleum

(BP), Lord Simon of Highbury, as the Minister for Trade and Competitiveness in Europe within the Department of Trade and Industry.

To the legislature

The leadership of most parties maintains tight control over the selection of candidates to fight elections. In the Labour Party, its governing body, the National Executive Committee, compiles a shortlist of approved candidates for each constituency from which the Constituency Labour Party selects its preferred candidate. The Conservatives allow constituency associations greater autonomy, but they have taken steps to ensure the 'right' kind of candidate is selected. These measures have included:

- *In 1998:* New Ethics and Integrity Committee established with the power to remove unsuitable members.
- *In 2006:* David Cameron created an 'A-list' of parliamentary candidates for seats that the Conservatives currently hold, or hope to win, and introduced measures to increase the number of female candidates. A further change brought the introduction of US-style primaries for smaller constituency associations, with local voters given the opportunity to select the Conservative candidate from a shortlist.

The Liberal Democrats, meanwhile, allow the state parties (English, Scottish, Welsh) to establish their own criteria for selecting candidates.

To the bureaucracy

Although the civil service is in theory neutral with no party affiliations, ruling parties have long been accused of either making overtly political appointments, or subverting the civil service through the creation of discrete political units. The introduction of executive agencies after the Conservative civil service reforms of the 1980s saw fresh accusations that the people appointed to head the new agencies were recipients of political patronage. Indeed, a 2000 report by the Commissioner for Public Appointments claimed that two-thirds of British people think politicians stuff public bodies with 'cronies' and sympathisers.

Tony Blair's administration has come under fire for dramatically increasing the number of special advisers in civil service departments. This increase has been controversial because the advisers are both distinctly political and at the same time unaccountable to parliament. In some cases, advisers also have the authority to direct the action of civil servants.

Learning point
Are there any realistic alternatives to political parties?

Aggregation of interests and elaboration of policies

Most political parties are formed with the intention of representing the views of different groups or to articulate certain political ideas. However, it is not unusual to find parties which contain competing interests. As we have seen, the Labour Party has witnessed intense debate about the role of the state, while the Conservatives have struggled to adopt a universally accepted policy on the euro.

During election campaigns, parties produce manifestos that represent the programme which the parties wish to implement once elected. They also outline their vision of society. Construction of these programmes necessarily involves the *aggregation* of these competing interests into a coherent whole. Failing to do so may prevent a party from presenting a clear image to the electorate and, in the long term, undermine voters' identification with the party. Naturally, it is easier for parties with a narrower focus to aggregate the various interests which may exist.

The ability of parties to articulate and aggregate interests can be undermined in a number of ways:

(1) Powerful blocs can limit the ability of the leadership to make or implement policy. John Major's administration (1992–97) struggled to get its official policy on European Monetary Union (EMU) accepted by a substantial number of MPs, parliamentary candidates and even members of his cabinet.

(2) As outlined in Chapter 2, broader contextual factors can have an impact on the freedom to make policy. These factors might include the condition of the economy, nationally and globally, and electoral necessity.

(3) In coalition government, it is unlikely that one party will dominate to the extent that it will implement the whole of its manifesto. As a result, parties are forced to compromise their own policy interests in order to keep the governing coalition in place. After the 2003 elections in Scotland, the Labour and Liberal Democratic parties came to an agreement over their policy programme for the 4-year period until the next devolved elections. In this case, only two out of Labour's 242 manifesto promises failed to make it in to the 47-page agreement.

Feedback and communication

Political parties provide a means for information to flow two ways: from the political elites to voters, and from the voters to political elites (Figure 3.2).

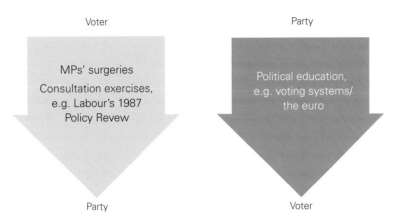

Figure 3.2 Flow of information between voters and political elites

If a government appears desperately out of touch with public opinion, opposition parties can also communicate this point through ministerial question time or parliamentary debates.

In practice, it is questionable how effective parties are in performing this function. Many would argue that the media and opinion pollsters (which may, of course, be conducting research for a party) provide a clearer picture of public feeling.

Encouraging participation in the political process

Parties encourage widespread participation in the political process. Whether it be participating in policy making through processes such as Labour's National Policy Forum; voting on a party's statement of aims (as Conservatives did on *Built to Last*); or helping to elect the new leader of the party (as Liberal Democrat members were able to do in 2006), citizens are provided with genuine opportunities to participate in the process through membership of a political party.

Of course, the extent to which ordinary members do have an influence within a party is open to question and is discussed in more detail below.

Task 3.1

It might sound a little disparaging to say this about people's lives and their problems and we did deal with them…but I got no satisfaction from this at all. I really didn't.

Task 3.1 (continued)

And all you were was a sort of high-powered social worker and perhaps not even a good one. So I won't miss that…

> Tony Banks MP, speaking to BBC Radio 4's *Week in Westminster*,
> November 2004

I never get bored, I always thought it was a real test of any MP's understanding of a community and their commitment.

I am elected by the community and answerable to the community. I am at their service.

> Simon Hughes MP (commenting on Tony Banks's view of MPs'
> constituent surgeries)

(a) What do the observations presented above suggest about the value of MPs' surgeries as means of informing political parties about public opinion?

(b) How far does the loyalty of an MP to his/her party conflict with his/her role as constituency representative?

Guidance

(a) They present diverging opinions on the value of MPs' surgeries. Clearly, Tony Banks regarded them as a waste of time, believing that constituents used them to moan about issues which MPs did not have the power, or interest, to tackle. Simon Hughes, on the other hand, sees them as an effective way to allow the public to hold him to account, and for him to be able to represent their interests more effectively.

(b) This is the one of the classic dilemmas of modern representative democracy: who does the MP represent? In some regards, there should not be any conflict. If the party loses sight of what ordinary voters want, then the MP is likely to lose his/her seat anyway. In reality, the pressures of the three-line whip and the desire for promotion within the party, coupled with the tendency of voters to support parties rather than individual candidates, and the single-member nature of UK constituencies, means that the loyalty of an MP today most frequently lies with his/her party.

How democratically are parties run?

The history of party organisation has tended to emphasise the extent to which most modern political parties are essentially top-down institutions, with power remaining in the hands of party elites.

> **Box 3.1**
> **Are parties run democratically?**
>
> **Robert Michel (1911) *Political Parties***
> Michel argued that an 'iron law of oligarchy' existed in all major parties. Writing from the standpoint of a disappointed socialist, he was attempting to analyse the structure of the German SPD. His conclusion was that, in practice, the major decisions were made by the party leadership.
>
> **Robert McKenzie (1955) *British Political Parties***
> In spite of their differing value systems and internal organisations, McKenzie believed that all major parties are dominated by the leadership. This is a necessary evil in order to prevent radical activists imposing an extremist programme on the party. It allows the leadership greater flexibility to respond to events.
>
> **Richard Katz and Peter Mair (1995) 'Changing models of party organization and party democracy: the emergence of the cartel party', *Party Politics*, Vol. 1**
> Katz and Mair argued that a **cartel** existed on two levels. First, it existed between the major parties in order to prevent the emergence of challenges to their hegemony. Second, it could be found on an organisational level, where a ruling cartel is responsible for financing the party and constructing its policy programme.

The pessimistic views on the state of internal party democracy in Box 3.1 need to be assessed through an examination of the distribution of power in the three main UK parties. Each party has claimed either to be democratically organised or to have made significant progress to becoming more open and democratic. In order to evaluate the credibility of these claims, three criteria are used for each party:

(1) What is the role of the membership in making policy?

(2) What is the role of the membership in electing and removing the leader?

(3) How is the party financed? (While not technically a feature of the party organisation, the means parties use to fund their activities is indicative of how democratic a party is. If a party is almost entirely funded by subscriptions from its membership, one could argue that it is likely to be more responsive to the wishes of its membership. If, on the other hand, it relies heavily on donations and loans from extra-party sources, then the leadership will feel less of an obligation to take heed of the attitudes and desires of its members.)

Labour

Based on a federal structure, the democratic credentials of the Labour Party are historically strong. Power was divided between various bodies, with ultimate responsibility resting with the party conference — the parliament of the party.

Table 3.1 shows the composition and roles of the main institutions in the Labour Party.

Table 3.1 Institutions of the Labour Party, composition and roles

	Roles	Composition
Conference	<ul><li>Makes policy resolutions.</li><li>Elects the NEC.</li><li>Exclusive power to reform the party Constitution.</li></ul>	<ul><li>Delegates from each constituency party, members of the PLP, union leaders (until 1993, union bosses gave the votes of their union as a 'block', thus giving them considerable influence at conference).</li></ul>
National Executive Committee (NEC)	<ul><li>Helps shape policy.</li><li>Responsible for party finances.</li><li>Maintains discipline in the party.</li><li>Helps select candidates.</li><li>Coordinates work of party outside parliament.</li></ul>	<ul><li>Around 29 members (including the leader and deputy and representatives from the unions, constituency parties, and various socialist societies).</li></ul>
Parliamentary Labour Party (PLP)	<ul><li>Represents the party in parliament.</li><li>Elects the shadow cabinet.</li></ul>	
Constituency Labour parties (CLP)	<ul><li>Select parliamentary candidates.</li><li>Secure the election of Labour candidates.</li><li>Part of electoral college to elect the leader and deputy (since 1980).</li><li>Select delegates to conference.</li><li>Vote for members of the NEC.</li></ul>	<ul><li>Individual members of the party and affiliated organisations such as union branches or the Fabians.</li></ul>

What is the role of the membership in making policy?

Until the publication of the 1997 document *Partnership into Power*, the Labour leadership paid little attention to the issue of the membership's role in the structure of the party. On paper, at least, this document radically transformed the way decisions would be made. In future, all members of the party would be able to contribute to the policy-making process, making it more open and democratic (Box 3.2 and Figure 3.3).

Box 3.2

Members' contribution to policy making

Under the new arrangements, members are able to contribute to policy making in the following ways:

(1) Organise/attend a local policy forum

Local policy forums are policy consultation meetings open to all members (and in some cases the wider community). In small discussion groups, the forums analyse a particular policy issue.

(2) Use *Partnership into Power* to develop local manifestos

The new *Partnership into Power* encourages local parties working with local government committees to consult residents and community groups as they work to develop the manifesto for local elections.

(3) Set up local policy networks

The new *Partnership in Power* proposals have outlined plans to set up and support local policy networks, which will encourage members with a shared interest in a policy area to join together to trade knowledge, discuss solutions to problems and engage directly with policy commissions, ministers and other opinion formers.

(4) Join the Partnership in Power Coordinators Network

Members of the network will get support and advice from the regional and national party to help run local policy forums, be invited to special briefing and training events and provide a platform to feedback to the party some of the political and organisational issues that arise through local policy development work.

Source: www.labour.org.uk

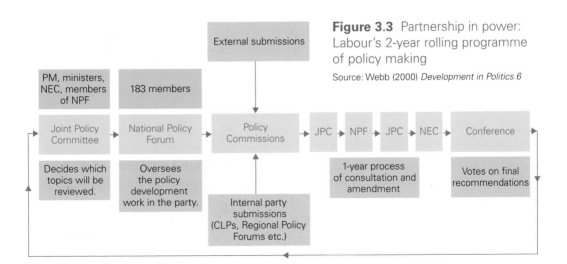

Figure 3.3 Partnership in power: Labour's 2-year rolling programme of policy making

Source: Webb (2000) *Development in Politics 6*

The membership was also given a role in the reform of Clause IV of the Party Constitution. In 1995, Blair held a plebiscite of all members on the issue; a process he repeated when he asked members for their approval of the 1997 general election manifesto. Criticisms of the way policy is made include:

- The Joint Policy Commission (JPC) is dominated by supporters of the leadership.
- The list of topics to be reviewed by the National Policy Forum (NPF) is decided only by the JPC.
- Policy documents are constantly referred back to the JPC, thus allowing the leadership plenty of opportunity to moderate their content.
- JPC and NPF meetings take place in secret, thus denying the membership information about how the final decisions are made.
- Blair's two internal plebiscites allowed him to make a direct appeal to all ordinary members, not just to CLP activists, who were likely to be more critical of party policy.
- No vote was offered on either the 2001 or the 2005 manifestos.
- Conference has been reduced to the status of 'rubber stamp' on policies decided elsewhere. It has to vote on policy reforms as a package and cannot reject individual sections. The party leadership has also made it clear that it will ignore conference votes which challenge official party policy. During the 2005 conference, delegates voted to support a return to secondary industrial action, the restoration of the link between the state pension and earnings, and limiting the involvement of the private sector in the running of the health service. None of these votes, however, had any impact on government policy.
- The leadership is reluctant to allow the kind of criticisms from the floor of conference which were a regular feature of pre-modernisation Labour. Activist Walter Wolfgang was temporarily ejected from the 2005 conference by security staff because he was heckling foreign secretary Jack Straw's speech. Grimsby MP Austin Mitchell had his digital camera confiscated shortly after, giving rise to accusations that the leadership was becoming more authoritarian in its management of the party.

Walter Wolfgang being escorted from the 2005 Labour Party conference by police officers

What is the role of the membership in electing and removing the leader?

Until the 1980 Special Conference at Wembley Arena, election of the party leader was solely in the hands of the PLP. Frustrated by the failure of the leadership to represent the wishes of the party during successive periods in office, conference voted to broaden the electorate through the introduction of an electoral college. The college would consist of three sections: the PLP, unions and CLPs, with the PLP and CLP each contributing 30% of the overall vote, and the trade unions 40%. By the time that the party required a new leader to replace the late John Smith in 1994, two changes had been made to the electoral college. First, ordinary members could now vote as individuals, rather than contributing to the CLP vote and, second, the balance had shifted away from the trade unions so that each section contributed a third of the overall vote.

On the face of it, these reforms have given more power to the membership. Yet, as Table 3.2 shows, when you consider the relative size of each part of the college, it becomes clear that the distribution of power in the college is not exactly even.

| Table 3.2 | Some voters are more equal than others: the electoral college |

	Size of college	% of overall vote per individual in the college
PLP and MEPs	353 + 19 = 372	33%/372 = 0.0887
Ordinary members	201,374	33%/201,374 = 0.0001
Trade unions	c. 2,000,000	33%/2,000,000 = 0.00001

The college has also been criticised on other grounds:

- It is an expensive voting system. In 1994, two unions decided that they could not afford to ballot their members so they did not participate in the election.
- The extent of union participation was further hampered by low turnout among union members and by the large number of spoilt papers in the union section. This was mostly due to voters failing to tick the box stating that they supported the Labour Party.

The ability of the membership to elect its leaders has also been undermined by the selective deployment of the *block vote*. Although replaced in 1993 by 'one member, one vote' at conference, Blair allowed union leaders to cast the votes of their unions in one direction in the leadership battles for the Welsh Assembly and in selecting the London mayoral candidate in 1998. This prevented the selection of candidates with significant local popularity, but without a record of total loyalty to the leadership.

How is the party financed?

The Labour Party has traditionally relied heavily on contributions from the trade unions. This was a result of historical factors — Labour was, after all, established as a party to 'represent the working man' in parliament — but also for practical reasons. Many thousands of members did not pay, or paid reduced subscription fees, preventing the party from being financed mostly by member contributions.

However, as the role of the union movement in the party as a whole has declined, so has the proportion of its contributions to overall Labour funds. In 1983, the unions provided 96% of the party's income, yet by 2002 the figure was 27%. Does this mean that the party has thrown off the influence of union bosses and reinvented itself as a member-driven party? In order to compensate for falling union contributions, and in an attempt to make the party appear more business friendly, much greater emphasis has been placed on raising donations and loans from the business community. Labour's courting of this sector has resulted in 20% of the party's income being derived from business. An additional 35% of its income comes from 500,000 'ad hoc' donations from ordinary members.

But has this undermined democracy within the party? Some claim that there is a link between the party's benefactors, and the policies it has pursued while in power. On a grand scale, one could point to a much more business-orientated approach to the economy than one might have expected from a Labour government. Individual cases also point to the power that money can buy. In 1997, it emerged that the Labour Party had accepted a £1m donation from Formula 1 chief Bernie Ecclestone, at a time when his sport was granted exemption from the ban on tobacco advertising. Labour continued to be dogged by accusations of selling access for cash. Paul Drayson, owner of vaccine company Powderject, provided over £1m for party funds in 2001–05. In 2002, Powderject was given a £32m contract by the NHS, and Drayson was made a life peer in 2004. Following an investigation into the appointment of peers, Tony Blair was accused of 'selling peerages' after four businessmen who gave Labour £4.5m in unpublicised loans were subsequently nominated for peerages. Ron Aldridge loaned money to Labour during 2005: he is executive chair of IT support firm Capita, which has won millions of pounds worth of government contracts.

When viewed in parallel with the changes made to the policy-making process, it would not be unreasonable to suggest that the cultivation of the corporate world provides several benefits for the party elites. If they can raise funds from outside the party, then they are not beholden to the wishes of the party when it comes to making policy.

The flipside to this, according to supporters of the leadership, is that without this approach, Labour might not be the election-winning machine which it is today.

Conservatives

Before 1997 it was technically impossible to talk about the organisation of the Conservative Party, as the party, theoretically at least, consisted of three separate bodies:

(1) **National Union of Conservative Associations.** Main roles included organising conference, supporting the parliamentary party and providing an outlet for the views of ordinary members to be heard.

(2) **The party in parliament (1964–97).** Solely responsible for electing the party leader. The position of the parliamentary party in relation to the rest of the party was remarkably dominant. Only when MPs committed a glaring political own goal did the associations dare to bring them to heel.

(3) **Conservative Central Office (CCO).** The 1997 election defeat not only reduced the size of the party in parliament, it also precipitated wholesale reform of how the party was structured, with the membership gaining a prominent role in the making of party policy and the election of the leader. How far this altered the balance of power in the party in reality is analysed below.

Learning point

Reaction and reform: William Hague's **Fresh Future** *(1998)*

- Created a single, unified party.
- Gave the CCO the right to intervene in association affairs.
- New method for electing the leader.
- Established policy forums.
- Endorsed by the membership in internal plebiscite.

In what ways were Hague's actions merely a response to the changes made to the Labour Party since 1994?

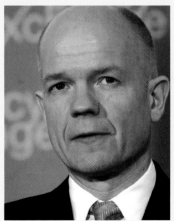

William Hague

What is the role of the membership in making policy?

If the Conservatives had good reason to believe that Labour's election victory was built on Conservative policies, then the Labour Party could claim that the 'favour' had been repaid when they saw the model of policy making introduced by William Hague in 1998. Using a relationship between the leadership, forums, associations and conference, it aimed to take a more inclusive approach, while maintaining a prominent guiding role for the leadership. As Figure 3.4 shows, members were given a greater say in making policy.

Figure 3.4 Policy making in the Conservative Party after the Hague reforms

According to Kelly (2001), the introduction of the Policy Forum heralded a new, more democratic, era in party policy making. He outlined several advantages to the new system:

- It encouraged a large number of members to participate in policy making (*c*. 5,000 1999–2001).
- Members of the party felt some ownership of the 2000 draft manifesto and constituency forums could point to specific ideas that they contributed.
- In some areas of policy, there was evidence that the leadership had changed its mind in response to feedback from the forums. He cites the dilution of the promise to restore the married person's tax allowance as an example of this.
- The policy forums played a not insignificant part in beefing up David Cameron's mission statement for the party, *Built to Last*. In an interview with the BBC, Cameron outlined the importance of local forums:

> They [party activists] liked it and they thought the aims and values were right but they said that we'd like to know more about what direction this would actually take a Conservative government in. So what we're doing today is publishing an updated version which, as well as the aims and values, actually gives a sense of direction as well.

Even so, one can refer to a number of arguments which are more critical of the extent of democracy within the Conservative Party's policy-making process:

- Some Tory activists regarded the Policy Forum as a superficial exercise in intra-party democracy, arguing that the leadership decided on the policy areas, submitted the original paper to be discussed and only gave members the opportunity to comment on, not initiate, policy.
- Under Iain Duncan-Smith and Michael Howard the ability of members to contribute to policy making was actually reduced. Duncan-Smith downgraded the role of the Policy Forum, while Howard allowed no consultation of the 2005 manifesto (in marked contrast to 2001). Some idea of the work of the forums under Howard can be gained from the following description of the 2005 Spring Forum, taken from John Strafford's (chair of the Campaign for Conservative Democracy) blog:

> I am afraid the rest of the Forum was what has become the usual junk. Rehearsed questions to Shadow Ministers who have rehearsed the answers — boring. Then we had the great audience participation exercise when a member could speak for two whole minutes on the good things that were happening in his or her constituency. There were not many takers. In fact, so desperate were the platform to get speakers at all, messages were sent to anybody to try and get them to speak. The result was that one speaker made the same speech to the Forum that he had made to the Convention the previous day…
>
> Source: www.btinternet.com/~johnstrafford/archive05.htm

- Unlike the 2001 version, no consultation was allowed over the 2005 election manifesto.

What is the role of the membership in electing and removing the leader?

William Hague's election as party leader suggested that the party in parliament had become greatly out of touch with constituency associations. Although he proved the most popular candidate in the eyes of a much-reduced parliamentary party, contemporary surveys indicated that his defeated rival Ken Clarke was the preferred choice of association chairs. In an attempt to enhance the credibility of his position, Hague held a whole-party ballot on his leadership in October 1997 and introduced a new system for electing future leaders (Box 3.3).

Box 3.3

Electing the Conservative leader: the Hague model

Stage 1: Conservative MPs whittle range of candidates down to two, after several rounds of voting. (Candidate with fewest votes drops out until only two are left.)
Stage 2: Whole party decides between the two candidates. Campaign lasts approximately 3 weeks.

As the new system enlarges the electorate by several hundred thousand, it is inherently more democratic than the system used between 1965 and 1997. The party has come a long way since the days when a 'magic circle' of party grandees would settle on the new leader without recourse to an election of any kind. The most recent election contest also featured a new angle, which added to the system's democratic credentials. For the first time since the new rules were introduced, each candidate had to address the party conference directly. While it did not formally represent further democratisation of the party, it did signify recognition that it was the activists, rather than the parliamentary elites, who would ultimately decide who the next leader would be.

However, the choice placed before the membership is still in the hands of the parliamentary party; with only two candidates to vote for, it is a choice that is more restricted than for any of the other major parties. The elections of Iain Duncan-Smith and Michael Howard both raised questions about the democratic nature of the system. In the case of Duncan-Smith, he was elected leader by the membership although he was not the first choice of the party's MPs. The protracted battle with his rival Ken Clarke exposed the policy divisions within the party, and arguably created an impression of a party riven by faction and incapable of managing itself, let alone governing the country. Duncan-Smith failed to bring the party together after his election, and his downfall was probably sealed after a lacklustre conference in 2003.

Michael Howard's election emphasised the power of the MPs even under the new system. Perhaps wishing to avoid a bitter contest in the run-up to a general election, no other MPs declared against Howard. As a result, the membership was denied a vote on who should be the leader.

After announcing his decision to resign the leadership, following the defeat in May 2005, Michael Howard provoked a fierce backlash from party members when he submitted a proposal to return control over the process to the parliamentary party alone. Although 71% of MPs and interestingly 58% of activists supported his plan, he failed to get the two-thirds majority required to introduce the change. As a result, the contest to elect his successor took place under the rules which had governed his own election and that of Iain Duncan-Smith.

The role of the Constituency Associations in selecting parliamentary candidates has also come under attack in recent years. Before 1997, Central Office had little control over whom associations selected as their candidate, and when they had attempted to foist candidates on local parties, they invariably had to cede authority to the association concerned. However, the inability of the party leadership to remove scandal-hit Neil Hamilton as parliamentary candidate for Tatton in 1997 prompted an attack on local autonomy under the *Fresh Future* reforms. Under the new arrangements, any prospective candidate would have to match criteria set by a new Ethics and Integrity Committee; a body which might have prevented Hamilton from standing as a Conservative candidate in 1997. In the lead-up to the 2005 election, Adam Hilton was removed as prospective parliamentary candidate for Slough on the grounds that he would create embarrassing media coverage after he had written articles for *The Spectator* alleging papal influence in the EU.

New leader David Cameron has attempted to further diminish the independence of local associations in selecting parliamentary candidates. In December 2005, he announced plans to create an A-list of candidates who will eventually be selected for seats which Conservatives hope to win at the next election. Half the candidates on the list will be women. Cameron's intention is to make the party's candidates more representative of the diverse societies which they would have to represent, and, in the process, change people's perceptions of the party. He has not been afraid to take on local associations that defy the national party (Box 3.4).

Box 3.4

Response to Cameron's plans

Cameron's plans have not been universally welcomed by members of the party. For instance, David Burrowes (MP) remarked:

> What we need is much more effort on local determination, a wider choice of people, whether it be from the voluntary sector, people championing social justice issues, and issues we're all concerned about.

> But it has to be much more of that local dimension, with all that experience that comes from being a local champion for people.

> That's what people want. They don't so much want a celebrity or someone who's a beautiful person — they want someone who is going to be working hard locally, for the benefit of all.

Source: http://news.bbc.co.uk/1/hi/uk_politics/5029462.stm (June 2006)

Even so, some local associations have asserted their autonomy. The 2005 parliamentary candidate for Chester resigned after anti-modernisation activists in the constituency threatened to deselect him. Cameron's primary initiative has also faced opposition. In December 2006, Conservative activists in Plymouth and Sutton voted not to ratify the selection of Patrick Nicholson, despite his victory in the party primary.

In June 2006, the Bromley Constituency Association defied Central Office by ignoring the A-list and selecting a local man, Bob Neill, to defend the safe Conservative seat in a by-election following the death of the sitting MP Eric Forth.

However, there is evidence to suggest the scheme is not meeting its creator's aims. By September 2006, seven out of the 22 candidates selected were women, while just two were from minority ethnic backgrounds. Perhaps this is what prompted Cameron to announce further plans to reform the candidate selection process. At least two of the final prospective candidates would have to be women and, as outlined above, larger associations would be able to hold primaries to select the candidate (as experimented with in Warrington South before the 2005 general election) — thereby denying them one of their most important roles.

David Cameron's plans for the selection of the London mayoral candidate have also led to accusations of central control. First, a selection panel will decide on a list of prospective candidates and then a London-wide primary will be held to select the official Conservative candidate. This has proved controversial because not only will anyone wishing to vote in the primary be charged a small fee to do so, but control over the selection of the candidate will be taken out of members' hands. A further problem emerged when it became clear that the race to be the Conservative candidate had attracted only a mediocre field by the 4 August 2006 closing date. In order to give sufficiently exciting and media-friendly individuals the further opportunity to apply, the closing date was put back 6 months.

How is the party financed?

Given the ideology behind the party, it is unsurprising to learn that the bulk of Conservative income derives from individual and business donations. The Conservatives raise approximately 90% of their funds from these sources, with particular individuals providing substantial donations. The key issue, of course, is: has this had an impact on the direction of policy? The link between policy and donations is difficult to draw, but it is possible to see periods when large donations and policy have been closely linked. For example, multi-millionaire businessperson Paul Sykes has supported the party off and on depending on the nature of the party's approach to the EU. Although it is possible to argue that Sykes was responding to, and not dictating, Conservative policy, the party might be unwilling to lose his patronage at a time when the party is several million pounds in debt.

Spread-betting tycoon Stuart Wheeler, who donated £5m to the party in 1998, has not been a figure reluctant to use his financial leverage to apply pressure on party leaders. In October 2003, he publicly criticised Iain Duncan-Smith's leadership and called for the party to replace him. He subsequently made it clear that he would not support a party led by Ken Clarke.

The scale of these donations raises serious questions about the independence of party leaders. As Liberal Democrat Malcolm Bruce commented in 2001: 'When individuals make such large donations, their expectations of influence can't be ignored.' Stuart Wheeler came close to agreeing with this point in an interview with the BBC in 2004: 'Of course you have got much better access but that is just life. There is nothing wrong with that.'

In March 2006, David Cameron attempted to deflect criticism of the party's reliance on large donors, and its reluctance to publish the list of donors and lenders, by putting forward his own proposals on party funding. These included a ban on all loans unless from financial institutions on fully commercial terms and a £50,000 cap on donations.

Liberal Democrats

What is the role of the membership in making policy?

The Liberal Democrats, like Labour, are organised in a federal structure, but its nature and workings are different. At the top of the structure is the national federal party, which makes policy on those issues that affect the whole of the UK. Beneath this are three state parties (English, Welsh and Scottish) and a number of regional and local parties (see Figure 3.5). Where legislation is made at a sub-national level, in Scotland for example, the corresponding branch of the federal structure is responsible for relevant policy.

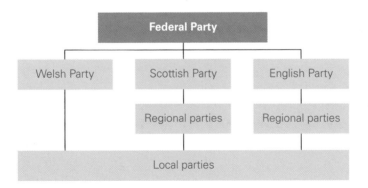

Figure 3.5 The federal structure of the Liberal Party
Source: www.libdems.org.uk/party/structure/

As Figure 3.6 shows, the role of ordinary members in influencing Liberal Democrat policy is substantial. Policy is initiated by either the Federal Conference or the Federal Policy Committee (FPC), most of whose members are elected by representatives at conference.

Chapter 3

Figure 3.6 Liberal Democrat policy making

The case that Liberal Democrat members enjoy a greater role in determining policy than counterparts in other parties is a strong one:

- Members have an extensive role in selecting members of the FPC.
- Party members send delegates to conference, which is the sovereign body of the party.
- Kelly (2005) points to the refinement of the party's policy on a local income tax as an example where the final version was markedly different from the original FPC proposal.
- The September 2005 conference provided several examples of conference voting to send proposals back to the FPC for further consideration. These included opposition to the privatisation of Royal Mail (which the leadership supported) and the imposition of a cap on the EU budget.
- Fearful of a revolt by activists over plans to drop the upper tax rate of 50% during the autumn 2006 conference, party officials decided to offer conference a straight vote on the issue. They hoped that this would prevent activists introducing and passing their own motion to keep it, which would effectively leave the leadership with two conflicting economic policies.

However, that is not to say that the party elites are completely powerless:

- Former leader Paddy Ashdown secretly negotiated a deal with Tony Blair before the 1997 election, the terms of which would have brought the Liberal Democrats into a coalition government if Labour lacked a decisive overall majority.
- Charles Kennedy relied heavily on a close-knit group of colleagues when producing the 2005 manifesto.

What is the role of the membership in electing and removing the leader?

Every party member has the right to participate in the election of the party leader and the party president. The election takes place using the single transferable vote system (STV), which, its supporters claim, contributes further to the democratic nature of the contest. Using STV minimises the number of wasted votes as voters are allowed to indicate a rank order of preferences. If a voter's first-choice candidate is eliminated, as Simon Hughes was in the first round, then the second choices of people who voted for him are redistributed in the second round (Table 3.3). Parliamentary, Scottish Parliament, Welsh Assembly and London Mayoral candidates are also selected using the STV.

| Table 3.3 | Electing the Liberal Democrat leader |

	First round votes %		Second round votes %	
Menzies Campbell	23,264	45	29,697	58
Simon Hughes	12,081	23		
Chris Huhne	16,691	32	21,628	42
Turnout	52,036	72	(1999: 62%)	

The only way in which the party leadership has intervened in the method for selecting parliamentary candidates in recent years was with the introduction of a quota for the number of women on the shortlist. Under the new rules one-third of the prospective candidates on the shortlist have to be women.

How is the party financed?

The Liberal Democrats rely on donations from large institutions and generous benefactors to a much lesser extent than either the Labour or Conservative parties. Most of the party's income comes from individual members, constituency parties and affiliated bodies. Even so, the party's method of paying for the 2005 general election campaign indicated that it was moving slowly to the fund-raising models adopted by their bigger political rivals. Of the £6m spent by the Liberal Democrats on the campaign, more than £3m was raised through donations. The biggest donation was provided by a company owned by Michael Brown, a Scottish businessman, whose firm operates out of Switzerland.

Learning point

Although the party was cleared by the Electoral Commission of breaking rules regarding acceptance of donations from foreign nationals or companies not based in the UK, the size of the donation still raised questions about the balance between the role of the leadership and party members in directing the party.

Why should foreign nationals not be allowed to donate money to UK political parties?

Task 3.2

Major donors to political parties, 2005

- Lord Sainsbury: £2.5m to Labour.
- Michael Brown: £2.4m to Liberal Democrats.

(a) In what ways does the reliance on such donations make the parties any less democratic?

(b) Make a case for the introduction of state funding of political parties.

Task 3.2 (continued)

Guidance

(a) There is circumstantial evidence that money buys influence (Ecclestone; Hinduja; Lord Sainsbury; Wheeler), while there has been a suggestion that it also buys you titles (Aldridge et al.). It undermines any claims about internal party democracy, as party elites do not have to rely on the membership for funding, which gives them a freer hand when it comes to deciding on party policy.

(b) At present, the Liberal Democrats are at a disadvantage as they do not receive as much from large donors as Labour and the Conservatives. Labour also benefits enormously from its union links. State funding removes suspicion of large donors buying influence with a party. It would prevent parties experiencing financial difficulties between elections — the Conservatives have to sell their headquarters at Smith Square in London to pay off a £2.5m pre-election loan. Finally, state funding would enable parties to devote more time to political education and policy research.

Conclusion

Political parties are essential to the preservation of liberal democracy in the UK. They offer citizens a means to participate in policy making and in the selection of our political leaders, and they provide a mechanism for the representation of different groups in society.

But how can our current party system offer any claim to be democratic? Voters do not have a real choice at the ballot box: the absence of political principles and the electoral system see to that. Furthermore, critics of political parties point to the increased distance between the parties and the public. Fewer people are prepared to vote for a party let alone join one. There is much evidence to suggest that even joining a party offers little opportunity to influence its direction. In spite of the changes introduced during the last decade, both major parties are as centralised and elite-dominated as they were in McKenzie's day.

But maybe McKenzie was right in his view that it is the very lack of internal party democracy which maintains the democratic nature of the political system as a whole. By keeping power away from activists, who tend to be more extremist than the leadership, and placing it in the hands of the elites, parties are actually making a massive contribution to the continuance of Britain's democratic tradition.

Task 3.3

Do the differing internal structures of the three main parties influence how democratic they are in practice?

Guidance

Michels, McKenzie and Katz would argue that all parties contain strong centralising tendencies, irrespective of their internal organisation. Activists are tolerated as a necessary evil, but are denied any real say in deciding the direction of the party. In each party, formal mechanisms for member participation exist, but even a cursory examination of the manifestos from 2005 would suggest that the input of ordinary members was token.

The methods of electing the party leaders partially challenge this view, with all main parties including a degree of membership participation. However, in each case, the balance of power remains with the party elites. In Labour's case, the unequal weighting of electoral college votes gives a dominant role to the parliamentary party and MEPs, while the final choice of candidate is determined by the parliamentary party in the case of the Conservative Party. Perhaps the Liberal Democrats offer the most open and equal election system, but even then, the candidates are all members of the parliamentary party, and the use of STV discriminates against the election of a radical leader.

Useful websites

- Revolts.co.uk (University of Hull-based site providing 'the definitive source for academic analysis of backbench behaviour in Britain') — www.revolts.co.uk/
- The Review of the Funding of Political Parties: Sir Hayden Phillips has been asked to work closely with the political parties and the Electoral Commission in order to produce recommendations on (i) the case for state funding of political parties, including whether it should be enhanced in return for a cap on the size of donations and (ii) the transparency of political parties' funding. He had to report to the government by the end of December 2006 with recommendations for any changes in the current arrangements — www.partyfundingreview.gov.uk/index.htm

Further reading

- Fisher, J. (2003) 'Party finance: new rules, same old story?', *Politics Review*, Vol. 12, No. 4.
- Kelly, R. (2005) 'Making party policy', *Politics Review*, Vol. 13, No. 4.

What makes a successful pressure group?

Conventional wisdom held that pressure groups with direct access to decision makers were far more likely to be successful in achieving their objectives than those who, for whatever reason, did not enjoy such contacts. However, in recent years considerable attention has been paid both to the shift in strategies deployed by several pressure groups and to the increased success of 'outsider' groups. This chapter examines the extent to which access equals success and outlines the principal reasons for the growth in direct-action groups since the early 1990s.

The insider/outsider approach: is it still valid?

The 'insider/outsider' typology is just one way to classify pressure groups. It was developed by Wyn Grant (2000) as an alternative to an earlier form of classification which based its distinction on the purpose of different groups: whether they were sectional or cause groups.

> **Sectional groups**
>
> Established to represent the interests of a common group of people.
> Example: British Medical Association (BMA)

> **Cause groups**
>
> Established to pursue specific issue goals.
> Example: Campaign for Nuclear Disarmament (CND)

The underlying assumption behind this typology was that sectional groups tended to enjoy insider status, while cause groups worked outside the network of ministers and civil servants. Grant argued that the sectional/cause typology did not offer a sufficiently tight method of classifying pressure groups.

- Cause groups can have either insider or outsider status. The Howard League for Penal Reform is an example of a cause group with both, as it attempts to influence government policy through campaigns, and also helps develop and implement policy. Its role in reducing suicides and self-harm among prisoners illustrates this dual role. After publishing several reports on the topic, it has subsequently worked with the Northern Ireland Prison Service to develop a strategy for preventing suicides and self-injury.
- Similarly, sectional outsider groups exist. This is particularly the case among groups representing elderly people. Given that this section of society maintains a heterogeneous complexion, it is difficult to organise its members into a single movement.
- Some sectional groups may choose to alternate between an insider and outsider strategy, depending on the issue or prevailing political context. The British Medical Association is one such group. While operating as a key actor in the creation and implementation of government health policy, it will also conduct public campaigns in order to influence the political agenda. This might involve criticisms of the very politicians who the BMA works with as valued insiders.

> **Learning point**
>
> *The BMA inside outside?*
>
> The BMA has campaigned against the following government policies:
> - legalisation of assisted suicide
> - targets for accident and emergency departments
> - reform of NHS pensions
> - extension of patient choice
>
> Does the twin-track policy pursued by the BMA strengthen or weaken its ability to influence government policy?

Grant (2000) offered an alternative typology based on the location of pressure groups in the policy-making process. This distinguished between groups on the *inside* of the process, with direct access to ministers and civil servants, and those who remained on the *outside* of it.

Characteristics of insider groups

- Insider groups possess credibility. That is to say they are recognised by the government as being representative of interests or issues. A group's authority is undermined in the eyes of the government when it splinters or a rival group emerges. This may explain the weakness of the teachers' unions, given that there are three main unions that disagree over key areas of education policy.

- They have particular political skills, such as awareness of the language used by the bureaucracy, and expert information about their area of interest. The Howard League for Penal Reform is often used as a good example of such a group.
- They are allowed to participate in the formal consultation process and, more importantly, the informal policy process.
- They agree to abide by the established protocol. This includes presentation of a well-researched, realistic case, acceptance of the final decision and selling the end result to their members. Ministers and civil servants are not impressed by groups that exaggerate the dangers of a particular policy to their members. A good track record of reliable advice is essential if a group wishes to maintain its insider status.

Three types of insider groups

The three types of insider groups are:

(1) **core:** cover a range of issues, e.g. National Farmers' Union

(2) **specialist:** focus on a specific issue, e.g. Greenpeace

(3) **peripheral:** groups with insider status but lacking influence, e.g. local authorities

---

Box 4.1

How do insider groups operate?

- Informal contacts with civil servants.
- Participate in official consultation exercises.
- Some will use the media to reinforce their negotiating position with ministers.

Characteristics of outsider groups

Outsider groups normally fall into one of two types.

Outsiders by necessity

This is usually because of the limited resources that a group has. For example, it may have only a small membership or it may lack the financial backing to maintain the staff and offices normally required to pursue an inside strategy. Alternatively, the group may not pursue goals which are compatible with the governing party, thus forcing it to use an outsider strategy. This was the case with the equal parenting pressure group Fathers 4 Justice, which failed to make an impact on government policy, so it adopted a strategy based around high-profile publicity stunts.

While some groups which fall into this category are resigned to their status, many others aspire to become insiders. Grant cites the gay rights group Stonewall as an example of an 'aspirational' outsider group. Using a combination of methods, including discreet ministerial-level meetings (sometimes using celebrities as an additional 'hook') and the maintenance of a small, professional office, Stonewall has been able to gain access to decision makers. Illustrating its change in status, Stonewall fought the Royal Navy in the European courts over the ban on gays in the military, yet now it works closely with the Navy to oversee the successful implementation of the legal judgement. It could also claim a role in the introduction of the Civil Partnership Act 2004.

Outsiders by choice

Other groups reject cooperation with ministers and civil servants for fear of having their goals compromised by the 'establishment'. Usually, these groups are more ideological in nature than other outsider pressure groups. By way of contrast with Stonewall, another gay rights group OutRage! relies on a small, committed group of radicals to publicise its cause using outrageous stunts (Box 4.2). These are intended to capture the attention of the media and their audience, in order to draw attention to certain issues. On Easter Sunday in 1998, for example, the group's leader and most prominent member, Peter Tatchell, and six other members of OutRage! invaded the Archbishop of Canterbury's pulpit and accused him of discriminating against homosexuals.

Box 4.2

What methods do outsider groups use?

Some of the most common tactics used by outsider groups have included:

- demonstrations
- advertisements in the media
- boycotts
- disruption
- lobbying parliament
- referendums
- standing for parliament
- international coordinated action
- petitions

Criticisms of Grant's typology

The four main criticisms of Grant's typology are detailed below.

Some groups are able to pursue insider and outsider strategies simultaneously

Indeed, many groups have been able to exploit government initiatives to widen the consultation process in policy making, while pursuing a classic outsider strategy. It may even help their cause to operate tactically on two levels. Greenpeace has long pursued what some have christened a 'wet suit' and 'business suit' approach. This pressure group has been happy to send U2 in a dinghy to protest against the effects of nuclear power, while negotiating with national and international administrations over the same issue.

Grant acknowledges the trend towards twin-track approaches, but claims that in the long run this could create tensions between activists and elites within groups.

It exaggerates the barriers to insider status

Recent studies have suggested that insiders outnumber outside groups to a large extent in certain policy areas. Page (2003) goes so far as to claim a 9:1 ratio. Certainly, the election of the Labour government has contributed to the increasing ease of access to the policy-making process. It has done so in three ways.

Cabinet Office Code of Practice on Consultation (2000)	Devolution to the regions	Use of think tanks to formulate policy
Aimed to open up decision making to all, if a new policy or if new regulation is planned. Emphasised the role of the internet in allowing groups to contribute to consultations.	First, it gave regional groups opportunities denied to them in the pre-devolution era. Second, the Scottish Civic Forum offered minority groups the chance to contribute to debates on social and civic issues. The Scottish Executive also encourages depart-ments to consult widely, across a range of groups.	In some ways, think tanks have replaced trade unions as the Labour Party's pressure group type of choice. Several members of think tanks have become either ministers or special advisers, and Tony Blair involved several think tanks in drawing up the 2005 manifesto.

Grant's response to this criticism is to point out that the opening-up of the process has not changed the criteria for groups to gain insider status. It has merely allowed more groups to submit their ideas to policy makers. Whether they are listened to or not is another matter entirely. In the consultation document *Civil Partnership — a framework for the legal recognition of same-sex couples*, well over 100 groups were consulted. These included OutRage! and Stonewall, as well as groups who objected to the introduction of civil partnerships. Using Grant's argument, the groups which had the greatest influence would still have been those fulfilling most of the criteria identified above.

It ignores the development of new social movements

Grant's typology appears to make certain assumptions about a group's membership, objectives and methods. The development of new social movements poses a serious challenge to the suitability of this form of categorisation.

Typically, new social movements have broad interests, usually being concerned with society's values rather than specific policy changes. The 'Clean Up TV' campaign, started in the 1970s, or a desire to protect the environment are two examples of this phenomenon.

New social movements are not restricted to single groups. A movement may consist of parties, pressure groups and mass protest. These movements lack high-profile leaders and frequently involve people adopting a lifestyle which is an extension of their political beliefs. Someone who buys 'green' or fair-trade products thus may be counted as part of the same broad environmental or anti-capitalist movements which also include civil disobedience as a tactic.

A Reclaim the Streets march in Liverpool

New social movements, while possessing a broad political agenda, are simply too fluid to be analysed using a method which focuses on membership. Similarly, by deliberately rejecting the traditional campaigning routes (such as lobbying major political parties or starting a pressure group) and embracing more theatrical approaches, they do not sit easily with an approach that dwells on a group's strategy.

The typology does not take account of different policy-making communities across government

Implicit in Grant's typology is an attempt to explain why certain pressure groups are more successful than others at influencing government policy. Although it is useful in providing a general explanation, its critics argue that the development of policy differs throughout government. Instead of offering a general analysis of pressure group success, they suggest that a range of *policy networks* exist across Whitehall. According to this approach, certain departments would work closely with one group (such as the old Ministry of Agriculture, Fisheries and Food with the National Farmers' Union, or the Department of Transport with the British Motor Federation), whereas other departments might draw on a much more diverse and, in some cases, conflicting, collection of groups (see Figure 4.1).

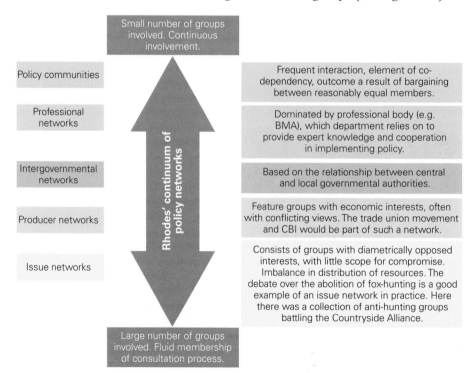

Figure 4.1 Rhodes' continuum of policy networks

The main advantage of using this model is that it allows you to develop a more accurate picture of where power lies throughout government.

Task 4.1

(a) Suggest reasons why Reclaim the Streets might reject an insider route.

(b) What are the main advantages to be obtained from gaining insider status?

Guidance

(a) The main reason would be that Reclaim the Streets rejects the system which demands that, in order to be effective, groups have to cosy up to ministers and civil servants. They also suppose that no government is ever likely to grant them insider status, so why bother attempting to gain it? Finally, the group is more concerned with changing attitudes than achieving narrow legislative successes.

(b) Pressure groups regard insider status as desirable principally so they can influence the policy agenda and/or the shape of proposed legislation. Once a measure has become law, the group may also play a significant role in how it is implemented. Of course, a small number of groups have insider status imposed on them, such as local government associations, yet feel this is actually rather constraining.

Are some outsider groups just as or more effective than some insider groups?

The rise in direct-action methods and the attention given to high-profile outsider groups such as the Countryside Alliance or Fathers 4 Justice have challenged previously held assumptions about the importance of 'access' for pressure groups. Most commentators would have agreed with Grant's underlying point — that access equals success — yet developments in recent years suggest that the importance of insider status is not what it once was.

The case for outsider effectiveness

Faced with competition from more radical pressure groups in their 'field', a small number of prominent insider groups have been compelled to broaden their strategies. A typical case is the National Farmers' Union. Grant refers to the

National Farmers' Union (NFU) as 'one of the best examples of an effective insider group', yet in recent years it has undergone a major rethink in its approach to the policy-making community. At a local level, members of the NFU have cooperated with the more radical Farmers for Action (FFA), a group which has adopted some of the more direct campaigning strategies deployed by farmers in Europe. The NFU has also cooperated occasionally with FFA in its attempts to defend the interests of dairy farmers. The NFU's changing relationship with government is symbolised by its decision in 2003 to move its offices from London to Warwickshire.

As Figure 4.2 shows, there is evidence that outsider groups are becoming more effective at influencing government policy.

> **Wales says 'no' to GM crops, March 2004**
> After coming under intense pressure from groups such as GM Free Cymru and the Farmers' Union of Wales, Welsh Environment Minister, Carwyn Jones, defied the UK government by announcing that Welsh farmers would be encouraged to declare themselves 'GM-free'.

> **Saving Shropshire's community hospitals**
> Community Hospitals Acting Nationally Together (CHANT) helped prevent the closure of Bridgnorth, Whitchurch and Ludlow community hospitals in 2006.

> **Shot at Dawn**
> John Hipkin, 80, organised the Shot at Dawn campaign after reading about a 17-year-old executed for desertion. Combining remembrance marches, lobbying Parliament and legal action, it succeeded, in August 2006, in persuading the MOD to issue a group pardon of over 300 soldiers who were shot for military offences during the First World War.

> **Jamie's dinners: Feed Me Better**
> Television chef Jamie Oliver used a Channel 4 programme and collected 271,677 signatures for a petition delivered to Downing Street. The DfES responded in May 2006 by reducing the amount of junk food in school dinners and investing more money in improving the diet of schoolchildren.

Figure 4.2 The effectiveness of outsider groups

Uncertainty over government attitudes towards insider groups

Although Labour has been keen to build a positive working relationship with business, it has, on the whole, become less enthusiastic about permitting pressure group influence in the policy-making process. Instead, the government has opened new channels of advice and information from focus groups, advisers, task forces and sporadic consultation exercises. On one level, this has opened the process to outsider groups, which are now able to overcome barriers to access. Government relations with the Confederation of British Industry have come a long way from the 'high point' of the corporatism of the 1970s, when it played an important role in setting government industrial policy. Since Labour came to power, the Department of Trade and Industry has preferred to deal directly with key players in the world of commerce. As indicated earlier, the introduction of a formal consultation procedure in Scotland has added to this process.

Increase in the use of direct-action techniques

'Direct action' refers to the process of deliberately campaigning outside the normal decision-making route and the targeting of the public (the consumers) rather than the decision-makers. By acting in this fashion, direct-action groups hope to change popular attitudes, which they believe will lead to more fundamental changes in society than enacting individual pieces of legislation. Although direct-action tactics are not exactly new (students of seventeenth-century England could doubtless reference the Diggers as practitioners of 'direct action') there has been a marked increase in the numbers of groups using these methods since the start of the 1990s.

Why has there been an increase in the use of direct-action tactics?

New technology

Numerous studies have suggested that the widespread availability and use of mobile telephones and computers have contributed to the rise in direct-action tactics significantly. On a practical level, the development of ICT, and the internet in particular, has drastically lowered the costs of participating in protest politics and has therefore increased the number of people participating in some form of pressure group activity. In some cases, it has also enabled groups to reach out to people who might not otherwise be regarded as likely supporters of that group. This theory was tested in a study of Countryside Alliance members and the extent to which they used ICT in their campaigns.

The CA seems to reach online an audience which is different from their traditional fieldsports base, an audience which is younger, slightly more engaged with the organisation, and might otherwise be more difficult to reach using traditional media.

Lusoli and Ward (2003) 'Hunting protesters: mobilisation, participation, and protest online in the Countryside Alliance'

Box 4.3

The importance of the web

The following submissions to the Power Inquiry also testify to the importance of the web in mobilising support.

John Gardiner (Deputy Chief Executive, Countryside Alliance)

In addition we have what we call the grass e-route, and that is the e-mail facility to get to tens of thousands of people. It is one of the reasons why we can press a button and within 24 hours' notice we can get 4,000 plus people to London, and with a few months' notice we can get half a million. In other words modern communication has inevitably enabled us to communicate more effectively and fast.

Adam Sampson (Director, Shelter)

Some of the most successful activity that's around at the moment and certainly activity that Shelter's trying to build on is built around the use of technology. The anti-Capitalist stuff is all fermented through the Internet. Shelter's campaigning increasingly is Internet driven.

The effects of technology have been most keenly felt by groups or individuals traditionally at the margins of politics. Practical uses such as information gathering or raising awareness of an issue have become much easier and quicker. However, the use of mobile phones and the web to arrange large demonstrations or meetings has had the greatest impact on the methods which certain groups use to gain publicity for their cause (Box 4.3). In the case of the Countryside Alliance march on London, Lusoli and Ward found that the web was the most popular source of information among people who used the internet about the march. In a number of cases, there was evidence that web-based pre-publicity resulted in people attending the march who probably would not have done so otherwise. Other research has found similar patterns among farmers and haulage contractors who blockaded oil refineries during the petrol protests of 2000. In this case, the mobile was the decisive tool in organising blockades across the country. According to the *Observer* newspaper, the mobile phone created a 'bush telegraph'; simply by contacting a dozen or so supporters, who in turn would contact a similar number, the leaders of the protest were able to mobilise hundreds of protesters in a short time. Clearly, the effectiveness of the technology in mobilising such large numbers depended on the existence of a network of supporters in the first place. However, immediate, mobile access to telecommunications was chiefly responsible for getting these contacts out to the oil refineries.

Learning from other countries

It is rare for protest movements to develop something entirely original. Usually, they adopt or adapt ideas and methods from protests that have already taken place. Most people will feel comfortable using methods that they have already tried or that have been successful elsewhere. Where direct action is concerned, many protest movements have borrowed tactics which have achieved results in other countries. The existence of global media and the development of ICT have made it easy to find examples of successful direct action beyond your own shores.

Several of the fuel protesters openly acknowledged their debt to French farmers:

> We looked at the French and we thought enough is enough…We are just doing it the same as they are. We are heartened by the fact that their protests are having an effect. We have to make sure ours does too.
>
> 'Blockade tactics cross the Channel', *Guardian*, 8 September 2000

> I know quite a few French farmers. Their union is far more in touch with everyday problems than the NFU, which is useless. They have a very tight network.
>
> *Guardian*, 12 September 2000

The proliferation of broad-based anti-capitalist groups has undoubtedly been influenced by the success of similar groups around the world. The high-profile activities of Reclaim the Streets, established in London in the early 1990s, spawned international versions of the group all over Europe, Australia, North America and Africa (Box 4.4).

Box 4.4

Reclaim the Streets and its brand of direct action

- Mass street party at a busy traffic junction.
- Shut down part of the London Underground by climbing on a train.
- 'Guerilla Gardening' outside parliament.
- Protesters take over part of the M41.

Exponents of direct action have clearly learned from the experience of other countries' *history*, or what they perceive to be the causes of historical change. An obvious example is the widespread global protests against the Iraq War, which

took place throughout 2002 and 2003. In many cases, protesters borrowed heavily from the methods and slogans of the anti-Vietnam war movement, which some claim was instrumental in forcing one president to resign from office and his successor to end the war.

Failure of established methods to achieve results

A common complaint of pressure groups is that their voice is never heard in the policy-making process. For some groups, the chosen way to address this problem is to keep on using conventional methods of influence, in the hope that they will eventually gain access. The environmental lobby groups Friends of the Earth and Greenpeace could be presented as examples of this reaction. Both groups have significantly moderated their strategies, moving from an overtly confrontational agenda in the 1970s, to one where they now work *with* business and government.

However, this approach has opened both groups up to the charge of being compromised in their stance on the environment because of their close links to the 'establishment'. Indeed, more radical environmental groups would argue that there is a real danger of pressure groups being 'captured' by government as soon as they attain insider status.

Groups that have their origins in radical forms of protest but have gained mass appeal also face a continuing tension between their desire to remain true to their original purpose and a desire to maintain a large membership, which is essential for income. One estimate puts Greenpeace International's global yearly revenue at $50 million, mostly derived from a membership of around 3 million people. However, the membership has fallen from a peak of 5 million during the 1980s, when the movement could also count on high-profile supporters such as Sting, U2 and Sir Elton John, who supported its 'save the rainforest' campaigns. One explanation for the decline in its membership was provided by one activist, who told the *Sunday Times* in 2000 that: 'The public is bored with seeing us chaining ourselves to ship and cranes.' In other words, its members supported its goals, but questioned several of its methods of achieving them. Thus, according to Doherty (1999), faced with the choice of alienating large parts of its membership or maintaining a radical campaigning front, it chose the former option.

The following comment on the London Rising Tide web-based forum provides an interesting, if somewhat direct, illustration of the frustration that some environmental activists feel about the established 'green' pressure groups:

> What…are Greenpeace playing at? Will they go the way of so many 'civil society' reformist movements? One has only to plot the trajectory of the repulsive Jonathan Porrit to get a glimpse of one potential future. This one time critic of capitalist depravity

has now become the suave prophet of business partnership, happily greenwashing his corporate customers at 'forum for the future', that's when he's not providing PR advice for the reactionary reptile Prince Charles or his war criminal buddy Tony Blair...

Source: www.londonrisingtide.org.uk/2005

Some activists also claim that the goals of such groups inevitably become more restricted: focusing more on specific legislative proposals, rather than the wider cultural changes that they argue are necessary to tackle environmental problems. To a certain extent, more radical groups highlight the capitalist system as being at the heart of the problem and by participating, and accepting the omnipotence of that system, moderate environmental groups are failing to address more fundamental issues.

As an alternative to seeking respectability, and the consequent dangers of compromise, groups such as Earth First! and Critical Mass have deliberately avoided using 'conventional' pressure-group tactics. Instead, they have adopted direct-action tactics to draw attention to their causes. Earth First! describes its general principles as 'non-hierarchical organisation and the use of direct action to confront, stop and eventually reverse the forces that are responsible for the destruction of the Earth and its inhabitants', and states that it has no central office, no members, no paid workers and no money. Although its reach is certainly global, it emphasises the importance of using local actions to achieve global targets.

Critical Mass, described on its website as 'an unorganised coincidence', organises cycle rides through cities in order to publicise alternatives to widespread car use. These take place on the last Friday of every month in locations around the world. Participants meet at the same location and time, and set about cycling through the city causing mild disruption, but with the emphasis on using bikes rather than cars.

A Critical Mass demonstration in London (2004)

Task 4.2

Do you agree with the view that the use of direct action is an admission of political weakness?

Guidance

In some cases, this is certainly true. Some groups resort to direct methods of protest because governments will not listen to them or because they have failed to attract the attention of the general public. The high-profile stunts of Fathers 4 Justice would appear to illustrate this particular line of argument, as would the activities of the anti-road lobby in the 1990s.

Even so, a significant number of groups reject any aspirations to insider status. Instead they use direct methods in order to force the public to question the values that underpin modern society. The mobilisation of the cycling community by Critical Mass is one such group. Other groups, such as Class War or Reclaim the Streets, reject the political system outright and feel that they would be compromised by conventional participation in it.

In some cases, direct action is used in parallel to more established methods of campaigning. The Manchester Education Committee has targeted directors and shareholders of Manchester United directly in order to apply pressure on them to resist the takeover of the club by the Glazer family. This tactic was used in conjunction with approaches taken by Shareholders United (organising a fans' buy-out) and the Independent Manchester United Supporters Association (lobbying supporters, Parliament and ministers).

Other pressure groups point to the failure of mainstream groups to prevent government policies being implemented. As a result, they have turned to direct action in order to achieve their goals. This does not automatically mean that they resort to conflict or large-scale demonstrations. In some cases, it has simply meant changing the focal point for pressure. For example, the evolution of the anti-road movement at the start of the 1990s was a direct result of the inability of earlier campaigners to prevent roads being built. Where previously groups had tended to rely on challenging the road programmes purely at the public inquiry stage, more recent protests attempted to act throughout the planning and construction process. This involved protesters occupying sections of land designated for road construction, which not only temporarily delayed the process, but invariably attracted considerable media attention. Although these protests were mostly unsuccessful, they did increase the costs of road construction and caused both major parties to rethink their approach to road building.

In 1994, the Standing Advisory Committee on Trunk Road Assessment reported that building more roads led to more congestion and was influential in persuading the Conservative government to rethink its policy. Three years later, the secretary of state for environment, transport and the regions, John Prescott, announced that he would have failed if the number of journeys by car had not fallen by the end of Labour's first term in office. He later established a 10-year transport plan, which stated that: 'There will be a strong presumption against schemes that would significantly affect environmentally sensitive sites or important species, habitats or landscapes.'

Learning point: the Dongas and the M3

In 1992, a small group of protesters occupied part of Twyford Down, in order to prevent it from being included in the extension of the M3.

Protesters on the site of the M3 extension at Twyford Down

How far do images of anti-road protesters, such as the Dongas (pictured above) deter people from joining campaigns?

One of the most ingenious forms of direct action practised by a group disillusioned by conventional methods of protest was demonstrated by a collection of Manchester United fans. They responded to the takeover of 'their' club by the US tycoon Malcolm Glazer by 'leaving' the club and forming their own version, F.C. United. The fans claimed that the club's shareholders and directors failed in their duty to protect it from an individual with no interest in the history or

traditions of the club. By acting in this way, the fans are not seeking to remove Glazer, but instead to offer disillusioned United fans the opportunity to support a version of their club that is based on a fan-centred model of ownership.

Conclusion

Most studies highlight the importance of three common factors that contribute to pressure-group success: (i) resources, (ii) access and (iii) circumstances. Of the three, resources would appear to be the most significant factor as the amount of financial muscle, size of membership or extent of technical expertise a group possesses will often enable it to gain access to ministers and civil servants, and also to react quickly and effectively to changing political and economic circumstances. Extensive resources will also enable a group to deploy a variety of techniques to get its point across. The contrasting fortunes of the trade unions and the business community since the end of the 1970s provide a fascinating illustration of this conclusion. Whereas membership, and therefore revenue, of unions has fallen dramatically and its privileged access to ministers has long since ended, business leaders have maintained their place in the decision-making process under three different prime ministers and two governing parties.

Direct-action tactics certainly prove effective in gaining media coverage, but there is little evidence that they have been successful in either reversing government decisions or inspiring wholesale changes in the attitudes and behaviour of people in the UK and abroad. Similarly, new forms of consultation have not rendered the old insider/outsider distinction obsolete. Although ministers may listen a little more, they continue to be influenced by well-resourced groups whom they consult frequently.

Task 4.3

Just how do you organise a picket, apparently with small numbers and overwhelmingly peaceful, and get the cooperation of the industry you target (like the powerful oil industry) — and the cooperation of the police, along with apparent widespread public support? Having done this, you virtually bring the nation to a standstill in a matter of days; you do not get arrested or beaten by riot police; and get to be number one news for days. You also get to dictate what goes in and out of your target industry and, while not actually physically stopping any trucks, you declare that your peaceful picket will prevent all but emergency service deliveries.

Source: anonymous e-mail from an animal rights activist commenting on the fuel protests, posted on closed email list, 14 September 2000

> ### Task 4.3 (continued)
>
> **(a)** How does this posting suggest that the success of pressure-group activity is heavily influenced by support from the political establishment?
>
> **(b)** How far do you agree with this view?
>
> #### Guidance
>
> **(a)** The author of this e-mail contrasts the official treatment of the fuel protesters with that of environmental campaigners. He suggests that the authorities were actually more lenient and patient with the group that was breaking the law and effectively holding the country to ransom for their own selfish needs than with campaigners who were attempting peacefully to change the government's mind about issues that affect the whole planet.
>
> **(b)** This argument is endorsed by elitists and Marxists, who claim that the power of capital and the shared interest of economic and political elites always result in victories for right-wing groups. By way of contrast, pluralists reject any notion of elitist protection. Instead, they argue that decisions are based on merit, and the extent to which groups actually represent the majority view.

Useful websites

- Action Network
  www.bbc.co.uk/dna/actionnetwork/C1269
- London Rising Tide
  www.londonrisingtide.org.uk/node/1

Further reading

- Grant, W. (2004) 'Pressure politics: the changing world of pressure groups', *Parliamentary Affairs*, Vol. 57, No. 2.
- Watts, D. (2006) 'Pressure group activity in post-devolution Scotland', *Talking Politics*, Vol. 18, No. 2.

Are pressure groups a threat to democracy?

It would appear somewhat perverse to regard anything that encouraged greater participation in politics as undemocratic. Furthermore, several studies suggest that the increasing popularity of pressure groups in recent years is a direct result of perceived failings in existing aspects of representative democracy. Pressure groups are therefore commonly seen as antidotes to undemocratic politics, rather than a cause of them.

However, your study of group activity thus far should have already helped you appreciate that the democratic credentials of pressure-group politics are worthy of much closer examination. This chapter aims to question the extent to which pressure groups add to the democratic nature of politics in the UK. It does this by focusing on the functions of groups, the degree of fair competition between them and the distribution of power within them, before finally asking whether the influence of pressure groups has been overstated.

Why do we need pressure groups?

Traditionally, pressure groups have performed a range of functions, which have involved filling gaps in those areas of politics not tackled by political parties. As a result of concern about the state of Britain's party system, the importance of pressure groups in the political system has increased.

The 'traditional' functions of pressure groups

- They provide a means of popular participation in national politics between elections.
- They provide a means of popular participation in local politics.
- They act as a source of specialist knowledge.
- They act as intermediaries between competing groups.
- They have an important social function.

Groups that deal with particular issues or interests tend to accumulate specialised expertise in their field. As a result, governments often consult these groups and, in return, sometimes provide partial funding. For example, the mental health groups MIND and Mencap both advise the government, which gives them approximately 20% of their income. In 2004, the government commissioned Mencap to coordinate a feasibility study into the viability of a National Centre for Early Intervention that would provide leadership and coordination to the fields of childhood disability and early intervention for disabled children from birth to age 5. The findings were presented to the government in March 2005.

Some pressure groups exist almost entirely to campaign on issues that the government would ordinarily wish to promote, but over which it faces significant opposition. The anti-smoking group ASH is a case in point. It receives almost two-thirds of its funding from the Department of Health and other government offices, while members of ASH are commissioned to produce reports for government departments. Similarly, impressed by the way the Jubilee 2000 coalition of groups generated support for abolishing Third World debt, Chancellor Gordon Brown encouraged the anti-poverty lobby to set up an alliance, the End Child Poverty campaign, to mobilise public support for the government's 20-year campaign to abolish child poverty.

Campaigning to end child poverty

Why have pressure groups increased in importance?

- Membership of political parties has fallen. Given the important roles parties play in the political system, this decline in membership has added significance.
- There is a perception that political parties no longer represent the interests of their members. As indicated earlier, growing centralisation of power within the parties, accompanying a move towards consumerist politics, has resulted in politically active people looking for new groups as an outlet for their beliefs.
- The development of 'new social movements' has led to increased numbers of people joining pressure groups and new forms of protest.

Are some pressure groups more equal than others?

Positive views of pressure groups emphasise the centrality of groups to the democratic process. According to this line of thought, modern liberal democracy fails to allow extensive popular participation in the political process: individuals' meaningful political participation is limited to one vote every few years (at national level), and between elections voters have little hold over decision makers. In an age when political parties fail to articulate the demands of voters, pressure groups therefore could be argued to play a critical role in remedying a serious democratic deficit. However, political scientists are divided over the extent to which the competition between rival groups is fair. By examining whether some groups are more equal than others, we can get to the heart of the relationship between pressure groups and democracy.

The most positive interpretation of pressure-group activity is commonly associated with pluralism. Pluralists argue that society consists of many groups representing different sections of the population that all have equal opportunity to shape government policy preferences. Indeed, Robert Dahl (1971), arguably the most prominent pluralist thinker, wrote that democracy could not exist without 'the continuing responsiveness of the government to the preferences of its citizens, considered as political equals'.

In a pluralist system, all groups have the potential to reach decision makers, with their ability to influence policy determined largely by the size of their membership, by how far the leadership of pressure groups consults their members (i.e. how far they represent popular opinion), and by the quality of the arguments that they put forward. By filtering the varied demands of society into something from which governments can select the most appropriate policies, pressure groups effectively replace political parties as the main agents of interest aggregation and articulating. In the process, they render the role of the state benign, acting merely as arbiter between the competing interests in society. In his seminal study of decision making in New Haven, Connecticut, Dahl (1961) went so far as to write: 'Most of the actions of government can be explained…as the result of struggles among groups with differing interests and varying resources of influence.'

This view of pressure-group activity has been attacked for adopting a naïve attitude to the role that vested interests play in distorting the balance of power between competing groups. Pluralists defend their position by admitting that not all groups and individuals possess equal power. Instead, they emphasise that power is *dispersed* between groups, thus preventing the emergence of a 'dominant group system'. Dahl argued that power was dispersed in several ways:

- It is relatively easy for individuals and groups to enter the political system. Liberal democracies impose few conditions on active political participation.
- While resources are not distributed equally between groups, those that are better off in some resources are invariably worse off in other areas. This often means that one 'influence resource' is effective in some issue areas or in some specific decisions; it is by no means as effective in all areas. (The notion of *issue networks*, dealt with in the previous chapter, is broadly compatible with this view.) In the case of the UK political system, this would account for the influence of business interests on issues such as the management of the economy, and the support pledged by Gordon Brown for the aims of Jubilee 2000 — something that might conflict with the interests of the business community.
- The pre-eminence of one group is also prevented by the tendency for opponents of successful groups to mobilise support into the form of a rival pressure group. This provides a countervailing balance to previously dominant groups and establishes an approximate balance of power between them. The development of trade unions, and their role in the corporatist state in pre-Thatcherite Britain, is often used as an example of such a countervailing power.
- Few groups are entirely lacking in influence resources. Even the smallest, impoverished campaign organisations have the ability to exert some influence, if they are able to exploit what few resources they possess. At the very least, they have the power to deny their votes and the votes of their supporters to political parties that ignore their position.
- Individuals are likely to be members of several groups, thus bringing a wide range of attitudes to bear on any single decision made by one of these groups. For example, if a businesswoman was a member of a group aiming to reform the system used to elect MPs, because she believed that Germany's economic miracle was chiefly attributable to the consensual style of politics resulting from the use of the Additional Member System, she may approach the question of which system should be introduced to replace Single Member Plurality from a different perspective from someone who passionately believed in the right of voters to have a free choice between candidates as well as parties. As a result, because individuals are members of several groups, the tensions within one pressure group often cause it to compromise with other groups in the political system — social consensus results.

Figure 5.1 shows that the pluralist belief in the equality of potential influence is challenged from both sides of the political spectrum.

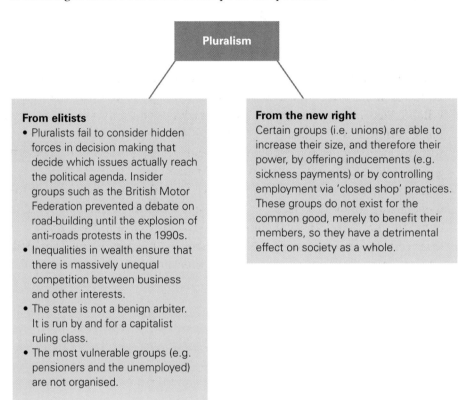

Pluralism

From elitists
- Pluralists fail to consider hidden forces in decision making that decide which issues actually reach the political agenda. Insider groups such as the British Motor Federation prevented a debate on road-building until the explosion of anti-roads protests in the 1990s.
- Inequalities in wealth ensure that there is massively unequal competition between business and other interests.
- The state is not a benign arbiter. It is run by and for a capitalist ruling class.
- The most vulnerable groups (e.g. pensioners and the unemployed) are not organised.

From the new right
Certain groups (i.e. unions) are able to increase their size, and therefore their power, by offering inducements (e.g. sickness payments) or by controlling employment via 'closed shop' practices. These groups do not exist for the common good, merely to benefit their members, so they have a detrimental effect on society as a whole.

Figure 5.1 Criticisms of pluralism

How far do pressure groups allow people to exercise power between elections?

If democracy is concerned chiefly with the exercise of power by the people, then pressure groups play an important role in ameliorating one of the biggest weaknesses of representative democracy: namely the lack of popular involvement in politics between elections. This argument presupposes two things, though. First, it assumes that members of an organisation are actively encouraged to play a part in most aspects of pressure-group activity: establishing policy priorities, fundraising, campaigning. Second, it assumes that governments are prepared to listen to and work with pressure groups.

Pressure groups as instruments of people power

- In theory, at least, groups provide a means for individuals to express their demands more effectively than they could do on their own. The World Wildlife Fund, with over 200,000 members, has a greater impact on government attitudes towards issues such as wildlife crime or animals threatened with extinction than a small group of individuals pestering the relevant government departments with letters and e-mails.
- Even the largest, professional groups have to maintain the support of the membership for their campaigns. To lose support means falling membership numbers and decreasing influence. Although they do not claim to be run democratically, groups such as Greenpeace or Amnesty International still rely on internal consultation exercises to keep the leadership in touch with membership opinion (Box 5.1).

Box 5.1

Amnesty International and membership consultation

Here in the UK we have a road show of meetings, eleven regional meetings around the country, with our members. We've had website contributions. We've had website discussions. We've taken this into our youth membership as well as our traditional membership organised around a regional basis and culminating in feeding back the response of all of that to our annual general meeting which then had further discussion and took decisions about the kinds of positions that we'd like the UK section of Amnesty to take into the international debate.

Source: Evidence submitted on campaign groups, Power Inquiry

- Defenders of pressure-group activity also state that groups increase access to the political system, ensuring that previously ignored issues are placed on the political agenda. Although its campaign achieved little legislative change, Fathers 4 Justice argued that its programme of high-profile stunts ensured that media coverage of the issue of family law increased by over 700%, and that government and opposition parties had to engage with an issue that had not been on the agenda before the group's formation in December 2002. Indeed, the founder of the movement has even been able to sell his account of the group's brief history to Miramax pictures, with a film already in production.

Fathers 4 Justice protesting at the Foreign Office

- Groups are also able to provide a 'quality control' mechanism on how policies are implemented by governments. After several groups (including Action Aid, Oxfam and Christian Aid) had criticised the debt relief package agreed at the Gleneagles G8 summit in 2005, Gordon Brown was forced to admit that not all the money pledged was entirely 'new'; much of it had already been pledged by individual governments.
- Pluralists argue that groups are essential features of modern democracies as they act as intermediaries between the ruled and the rulers, help disperse power within a political system and act as balances to undue concentrations of power.
- Robert Putnam argues in his book *Bowling Alone* that groups are a primary provider of social capital. This means that groups provide citizens with the means to interact with other people, which in turn helps to build mutual understanding and commitment and gain further social and political benefits. For example, by associating with a group, individuals may develop a range of transferable skills, such as negotiating or presenting. They will also be given an outlet for particular grievances and may therefore be able to influence the political agenda. Maloney (2006) summed up the social capital role of pressure groups as follows:

> Thus groups are seen as generators of social capital, engendering civic and political skills and democratic values; as such they act as an important lubricant for the 'proper' functioning of democracies.

Pressure groups as obstacles to people power

Class differences

Pressure groups tend to serve the interests of those members of society who are already over-represented, i.e. middle-class adults. With a greater emphasis on single-issue politics, and a decline in collectivist forms of participation, it appears that it is the professional classes who are gaining the most from pressure-group activity — both in terms of the skills developed and the political benefits accrued.

An article in the *British Medical Journal* about the lack of attention given to child injury prevention provides telling evidence about the possible consequences of this bias in pressure-group activity. The article, published in November 1998, highlighted the links between preventable child injuries and child mortality. Research at the University of Newcastle had also found that children from poorer communities were more likely to be injured, and thus more likely to die. The article concluded that a primary reason for the lack of government attention to this issue was the *shortage of pressure-group activity in this field.*

Research carried out by Li et al. in 2002 added weight to this argument, by demonstrating that the benefits of social capital were less likely to be felt by the lowest social groups (Figure 5.2).

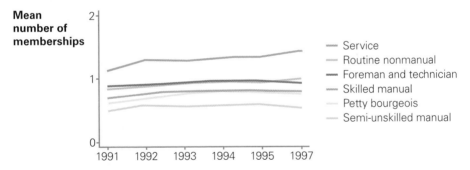

Figure 5.2 Class and social trends in social capital in Britain in the 1990s

The decline in union membership and activity since the mid-1980s has also contributed to the under-representation of the poorer classes, as the unions provided for many the only point of group membership. Li and Savage comment on the decline of *associational* membership in the following way:

> Since associational membership not only increases political participation, and hence political influence, but also delivers benefits of sociability including instrumental networks, we have further evidence of polarisation in British society where the most advantaged class is consolidating its privileges relative to the rest.

Learning point

Can you think of any other reasons why poorer members of society do not participate to the same extent as wealthier groups?

'Cheque book' groups

The emergence of 'cheque book' groups challenges the democratic credentials of group activity. These groups are run as hierarchical organisations, with professional staffers, researchers and campaigners. The role of the membership is merely to provide legitimacy to the group's goals and to bankroll the group's activities through membership fees and donations. In fact, some of these groups do not require the membership at all, as they rely heavily on patronage and have a sufficiently large team of expert campaigners.

Members identify with the aims of the group through symbols and media coverage, but experience little contact with fellow members, and hence receive little or no *social capital* from their membership. In a submission to the Power Inquiry, Professor David Marquand provided a critical view of some groups' claims to represent popular concerns:

> Greenpeace is more like a kind of company trading in the market place, and you don't join Greenpeace, you send it money and then you watch and see what it does and then you withdraw money if it doesn't do what you like.

'Cheque book' groups deliberately set out to limit member participation in their activities, for fear that it will lead to internal divisions and to undue media attention on more radical issues and positions that may be peripheral to the movement's broader strategy.

Other points

- Some groups are run by professionals on behalf of other people whose interests are not always directly served by the group leaders.
- Issue groups are reluctant to respond to changes in the mood of the membership and can resort to undemocratic methods in order to prevent a shift in their policies. After the Countryside Alliance attempted to infiltrate the RSPCA to reverse its anti-fox hunting stance, the board of the RSPCA responded by blocking the membership of up to 300 people thought to be blood-sport sympathisers or in pro-hunting groups like the Countryside Alliance.
- As shown in Figure 5.1, elitists argue that social and economic links between ministers and representatives of business undermine any pluralist notion of pressure-group democracy. Although governments might give the impression that they have consulted widely, and even perhaps introduced legislation which is hostile to the interests of their own class, in reality real power remains with the social and economic elites.

Task 5.1

Outline the main advantages to a pressure group of an active membership.

Guidance

(a) It helps the group claim that it is truly representative of its members.

(b) Active members are more likely to develop a deeper association with the group and may, as a result, offer a greater financial input.

(c) The ability to mobilise large numbers of supporters can create a more powerful impression in the media.

(d) An active membership may come up with a wider range of campaign strategies.

How and why has political activity changed in the UK?

Much literature has been devoted to the decline of citizen engagement with politics. Even the government has been moved to investigate new methods of encouraging people to become involved in politics: consultations, people's panels, regional assemblies, referendums, e-voting and even an online petition on the prime minister's own website have all been introduced to tackle this problem. This section considers how political activity has changed in recent years and attempts to provide an explanation for it.

The principal change in political activity has been a shift away from formal party politics, with large sections of the population appearing disillusioned or alienated with the established ways of participating in politics (Box 5.2).

Box 5.2
The decline of formal party politics

- Membership of political parties is falling.
- Turnout at elections hit record lows in 2001 and 2005.
- Identification with the major parties has weakened considerably.
- Support for single-issue candidates has increased (e.g. Martin Bell, Referendum Party, Richard Taylor, Bob Flynn).

More developed descriptions and explanations for this process are provided in Chapter 2. However, the decline in party-based activity masks a more worrying trend for those who point to groups as being *generators* of social

capital. According to Stoker (2006), participation in collectivist, or associational, groups is also in decline. This has affected working-class men in particular, as their primary form of group representation, the unions, has declined in size and influence. Since the start of the 1970s the percentage of men who are members of a trade union has almost halved, hand in hand with a large drop in the figures for membership of working men's or social clubs. The significance of this trend was picked upon by Putnam (2000), who stated that these types of institutions enabled men to combine 'individual fun with collective purpose'.

A range of contributory factors has led to this development, covering political, economic and cultural reasons. The attacks on the trade unions and the process of privatisation by Thatcher's Conservative government undoubtedly played their part in the decline in union membership, but so too did the long-term de-industrialisation of the British economy. This resulted in large numbers of workers either being made redundant or being forced to accept more flexible working conditions: two developments which the unions appeared powerless to prevent. Finally, a degree of embourgeoisement overtook sections of the working class during the 1980s, with the notion of 'popular capitalism' taking root among those who wanted to own their own home and purchase shares in the same companies that had recently been privatised.

In place of established patterns of political activity, the following four principal trends have emerged.

An increase in membership of campaign groups

The rise of pressure politics and campaign groups can be attributed to many causes. Arguably, the most important is the desire among members to do something about a single cause or narrow range of issues about which they feel strongly. This is regarded as more desirable than having to join a party and lending support to a broad canvas of policies, some of which they might not agree with. Individuals might also prefer the style of pressure-group politics, since it does not demand as much time and does not require them to develop a detailed knowledge of internal party policy-making procedure.

The erosion of traditional class-based rivalry might also have contributed to the popularity of group-based activity. The emergence of a dominant middle class and the de-ideologisation of British politics have arguably led traditional supporters of the major parties to weaken their attachments to parties and find an alternative outlet for their political beliefs. Given the intrinsically more focused approach of groups, they will offer the opportunity to maintain some form of political activity, focusing on an issue that the individual feels most strongly about. In this sense, citizens have become consumers in the political marketplace. Instead of visiting the supermarket to satisfy all their political needs, they are able to visit the high street and shop only in those places that focus on their concerns.

Greater willingness to take direct action

As noted earlier, the last decade has seen a greater willingness to engage in political protest. This has ranged from legal demonstrations (e.g. the NHS Together march in November 2006) to the kinds of illegal activity practised by animal-rights protesters, who have used intimidation to pressurise workers at Huntingdon Life Sciences and stop them carrying out their work.

Perhaps of equal interest is the use of political protest by groups that are not normally associated with left-wing causes. Neither Fathers 4 Justice nor the pro-hunting campaigners who stormed the floor of the House of Commons in September 2004 could be classed as traditional radicals.

The use of protest has also taken on an international dimension, with several examples of coordinated international protests occurring in recent years, including the Stop the War demonstrations in 2003. (Reasons for the increased use of direct action are dealt with at length in Chapter 4.)

'Cheque book' participation

The nature of cheque book participation has been outlined above, but why has it become an established type of group activity? Figure 5.3 illustrates some of the reasons why cheque book participation has become more established.

Figure 5.3 The group and its members: advantages of cheque book participation

A willingness to participate, but a reluctance to join

The upsurge in single-issue activity and new forms of political participation have not been accompanied by a willingness to join new types of political organisations. People are more likely to be associated with issues and protest movements rather than any single group. Indeed, campaigns such as Earth First! make a virtue out of the fact that there is no organisation as such, while Critical Mass's 'official' website actually denies being the official website. It is the concept rather than the organisation that people buy into, with their monthly cycle meetings being open to everyone.

Has the influence of pressure groups been overstated?

Inevitably, any study of pressure-group activity is going to carry with it the implicit assumption that pressure groups are central to the decision-making process in British politics. This assumption is enhanced by the case-study approach that many authors take when analysing the effectiveness of types of group. However, recent research places pressure groups as only one of an extensive array of participants in the policy process, and the actual ability of groups to influence policy depends on a number of outside factors. Heywood identifies the following four main criteria for pressure group effectiveness.

The political culture is conducive to pressure groups

The political culture of a state is likely to positively affect the importance of pressure groups if the answer to two key questions is 'yes':

(1) Are groups regarded as being legitimate, and their formation and participation in decision making encouraged?

(2) Does the political culture encourage people to join and participate in pressure-group activity?

Clearly, the answer to the first question is 'yes'. There is plenty of evidence to suggest that pressure groups do play some role in policy making.

- Governments allow certain groups to gain direct access to ministers and civil servants (i.e. achieve 'insider' status).
- Governments directly fund a number of groups.
- The Labour government has introduced consultation measures to increase access for pressure groups.
- Governments allow groups to be represented on quangos. For example, Jonathan Porritt, former director of Friends of the Earth and founder of the sustainable development group Forum for the Future, was appointed head of the sustainable development commission by Tony Blair in 2000. The commission also includes Anna Coote, former deputy director of the Institute for Public Policy Research, the centre-left think tank.
- At EU level, pressure groups are actively invited to lobby the Commission and Parliament.

Even so, elements of British political culture can still militate against pressure-group activity. A particular bugbear for many groups is the continued reluctance of government departments and agencies to comply fully with Freedom of Information legislation (Box 5.3).

Box 5.3

The culture of secrecy and pressure-group effectiveness

- The anti-bullying pressure group Bullying Online has said it is frustrated that publicly funded bodies are not covered by the Freedom of Information Act.
- Currently, requests for information that would cost more than £600 to process are disallowed.
- Friends of the Earth complained about 'cultural blockages' among civil servants that prevented information from being released.

• Even the contact details of civil servants are not freely available. Access to the Civil Service Year Book web page, billed as 'the official online directory for all government departments, executive agencies and related organisations' costs £70. It is actually an offence to make the log-in details freely available.

Pressure groups can also suffer if they are seen to be acting in a manner deemed out of step with the established culture of policy making. In October 2006, the Charity Commission (the non-ministerial government department that regulates registered charities) reprimanded Kurt Hoffman (director of the charity Shell Foundation) and James Smith (chairman of Shell UK) for lobbying Hilary Benn, the secretary of state for international development, at a private meeting in January 2006. The Shell Foundation, although given a £130 million grant by the multinational oil company Shell, is supposedly an independent foundation with an interest in promoting sustainable development among community groups.

The Labour Party's attitude to pressure groups has been somewhat mixed. While encouraging greater access to ministers and civil servants, and enhancing the role of think tanks, it has been wary about listening to pressure groups on two fronts. First, it has been reluctant to re-establish the close links to the union movement that previous Labour governments had. Second, it has been reluctant to be seen as a hostage to populist campaigning. Kavanagh has argued that a series of high-profile protests over disability benefits, taxes on fuel, rural life, university tuition fees and the war in Iraq have made the government more reluctant to listen to pressure groups.

With regard to the second of the two questions, participation in some form of pressure-group activity seems to be a popular way to get involved in politics. Pattie (2004) estimated that about one-third of the population were members of a group, excluding membership of motoring organisations such as the AA. Other evidence suggested that membership of groups and associations had grown by almost half between 1959 and 1990.

Although only a small percentage of the population appear to be members of *political* pressure groups, with most political groups having 2% or less of the population as members, 2% still translates as approximately 800,000 people, a significantly higher figure than the combined memberships of the Labour and Conservative parties. Membership of environmental, professional or animal-rights groups is at a higher level than that for political groups, thus supporting the view that the political culture encourages people to join pressure groups.

In terms of actual participation in some form of pressure-group activity, a less conclusive picture emerges. Whereas evidence points to a wide range of political activities, including several large-scale protests (the February 2003 march against the war in Iraq involved 1 million people), it also suggests that fewer collectivist acts are undertaken, with individual actions being much more commonplace (Table 5.1). Given the stated success of collective action, be it demonstrations or pickets, clearly this will influence the overall effectiveness of pressure-group activity.

Table 5.1 Patterns of activism in the UK 2001–02

Activity	Involvement (%)
Contacted politician	18.1
Worked in political party or action group	3.4
Signed petition	40.0
Took part in lawful demonstration	4.4
Took part in illegal protest	0.8
Donated money to political organisation or group	7.8

Source: *European Social Survey* (2002), reproduced in Stoker (2006)

Even so, the power of individual action should not be underestimated. If enough people act individually, the accumulated collective impact can be significant. In her evidence to the Power Inquiry, Harriet Lamb (executive director of Fairtrade) commented on the ability of people whose activity did not stretch beyond buying Fairtrade tea and coffee to make a difference:

> We all buy tea and coffee, and whatever the government decides to do, we can, in our little way, make a difference by the tea and coffee we buy, and at the same time by using this consumer power, not only would you enable us to make a difference and you'd make a difference here and there to the lives of actually millions of farmers, but you actually then bend the political will because we now can say to the government the public clearly want trade justice because they're ready to buy it every day…The main thing is that I think people are not aware enough of the power that they have.

The institutional structure is accessible

The significance of the institutional structure lies in its degree of accessibility to groups. In centralised political systems, there are naturally fewer points of access, in comparison with a federal or locally based system. The balance of power between groups and government will therefore be weighted heavily in favour of the government in a centralised system, as groups have a narrower range of allies to recruit to their campaign. In a devolved structure, groups may be able to enlist the support of regional assemblies or parties, which, in turn, might increase pressure on central government.

If a national government is affected by international legislation (e.g. from the EU), then the opportunity for groups to access the system obviously increases. In the case of the EU, there are numerous points of access (Figure 5.4). This maximises the potential for groups to be successful in trying to influence EU, and consequently UK, law.

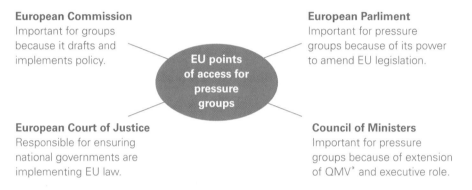

European Commission
Important for groups because it drafts and implements policy.

European Parliment
Important for pressure groups because of its power to amend EU legislation.

EU points of access for pressure groups

European Court of Justice
Responsible for ensuring national governments are implementing EU law.

Council of Ministers
Important for pressure groups because of extension of QMV* and executive role.

Figure 5.4 Points of access for pressure groups in the European Union
*QMV = qualified majority voting

A number of other factors contribute to the appeal of the EU for group activity. First, the EU holds a particular attraction for groups that are less likely to receive attention from domestic governments, hence the intense activities of environmental groups, trade unions and the Equal Opportunities Commission in the EU during the period of the last Conservative government.

Learning point
Lobbying the EU presents as many challenges as it does benefits for pressure groups. Do you agree?

The extension of policy competences for which the EU is responsible, moving from a focus on tariffs and trade to defence, fisheries, agriculture, immigration and social policy, has also greatly encouraged group activity at institutional level.

Most groups also recognise that a 'multi-channel' approach to lobbying is more likely to reap dividends. The EU offers the potential to target several elements of the European political system, on top of working at a national level.

Campaigning at EU level allows groups to develop alliances with similar groups from other member states. This increases their potential to influence the

Commission and the other institutions. A large number of British groups have joined 'Eurogroups', with the most prominent including the Union of Industries in Europe and the Committee of Professional Agricultural Organisations of the EU.

A further institutional factor may be the nature of the government departments. Departments are not set in stone, and all administrations are liable to rename or restructure them at will. The impact of such restructuring on groups could be significant. The National Farmers' Union traditionally enjoyed a strong relationship with the Ministry of Agriculture, Fisheries and Food. After its replacement with the Department for the Environment, Food and Rural Affairs, it struggled to maintain its influential position. By way of contrast, the creation of a department with responsibility for rural affairs provided a better opportunity for the Countryside Alliance to develop a dialogue with government, according to John Gardiner, the deputy chief executive of the Countryside Alliance.

The nature of the party system is favourable

In many ways, political parties and pressure groups are natural rivals. After all, they are, to an extent, chasing the same market of potential members, and both seek to set the policy agenda. However, each of the main parties has close links with a number of pressure groups and relies heavily on think tanks for much of their policy programmes.

The amount of influence that groups have over parties depends largely on the nature of the party system. Where a dominant-party system exists, groups inevitably focus their attentions on the party which holds power. In a multiparty system, the focus will be much more diverse.

The strength of party systems also contributes to the importance of pressure groups. In the USA, where party organisation is much weaker than in the UK, the power of interest groups is much greater. This can be witnessed from the reliance that candidates place on donations from Political Action Committees (groups set up to campaign for a particular candidate or cause), and from the impact that attack ads produced on behalf of PACs have on the fortunes of an election campaign. At least one president has blamed interest groups for his political demise. In 1980, President Jimmy Carter stated that single-issue campaign groups were at the root of his failure as a president.

The relative strengths of the UK party system have been discussed in Chapter 1, but the long-term erosion of the two-party system, partially explained by weakening partisan alignment, has had a profound impact on pressure campaign strategies. An increasing number of groups have entered candidates

for general and by-elections, with some groups achieving notable success. The experience of the Referendum Party in 1997 suggested that the electoral route was a viable one for groups aiming to embarrass the established parties and gain the attention of much of the electorate (Box 5.4). In Kidderminster, Dr Richard Taylor, campaigning on behalf of a group attempting to reverse the withdrawal of services from Kidderminster Hospital, not only defeated the sitting Labour MP in 2001, but also held onto the seat in 2005. Even the prime minister has not been exempt from being at the receiving end of this strategy: a founder member of Families against the War stood against Tony Blair in his own Sedgefield constituency in 2005. Although he did not win the seat, he received 10,000 votes and was given a national platform by the various media outlets during the campaign, especially when he delivered his vote of thanks to the returning officer.

Box 5.4

The Referendum Party and the 1997 general election

In 1996, billionaire businessman Sir James Goldsmith set up the Referendum Party to campaign on a single issue: for a referendum on the UK's continued membership of the EU.

Although technically a party, its single-issue focus gave it the appearance of a classic cause group. The formation of the party was a strategy rather than an intention to articulate a broad-based political philosophy.

Its impact was quite significant: David Davis suggested that the Referendum Party cost the Tories 30–50 seats at the 1997 election.

The nature and style of public policy are favourable

The nature and style of public policy influence the effectiveness of pressure groups in two ways. In the first instance, pressure group influence is likely to be greater when the government is prepared to intervene in economic and social life. When this is the case, business and labour groups have an incentive to lobby ministers in order to protect and further their own interests. Similarly, groups concerned with issues relating to the well-being of members of society, such as anti-smoking groups or medical associations, stand a better chance when the government is inclined to intervene in matters of daily living.

However, the direction of government policy, as well as the extent of intervention, is also critical in determining the importance of pressure groups in the political system. As indicated earlier, the Labour government has adopted a clear pro-business line, thus allowing groups such as the Confederation of British

Industry and the Institute of Directors more access to ministers than they might have expected from a Labour government, and one that rejected any return to corporatist government. In recent years, the government has taken a greater interest in overseas development, which, according to Steve Tibbett (Policy Officer, Action Aid), has resulted in much greater access to ministers and civil servants. Harriet Lamb from Fairtrade has also benefited from the government's desire to shape attitudes to development issues. Fairtrade has not only received regular grants from the Department of International Development, it has also received specific government funding to launch new projects such as 'Fairtrade Fortnight' and the accreditation of 'Fairtrade towns'.

A supermarket window display during Fairtrade Fortnight 2006

Assessing the importance of pressure groups is a tricky business. Pressure groups do not exist in a political vacuum; their importance is largely determined by the context in which they operate. They are not immune to being influenced by the very political system that they may be trying to reform or influence. For example, organised labour has moved away from reliance on strike activity as a result of legislation introduced during the 1980s. One of the difficulties in gauging the importance of groups is that the exact role that a group plays in influencing a decision is rarely clearly mapped out. Often a variety of actors and groups contribute to the policy process and the degree of influence of a single participant can be hard to fathom.

Conclusion

It is difficult to argue that the increased role of pressure groups has thrown democratic politics in the UK into crisis. They are, after all, probably the most popular means of engaging with the political system and offer a highly effective method of allowing individuals to participate in politics between elections. Membership is voluntary and comparatively few groups have specific bars on entry. Members are not obliged to sign up for a broad-based package, as they would have to in a political party. Therefore, groups offer the opportunity to participate, contribute and choose. In this sense, they contribute transparently to democracy being of the people, by the people and for the people.

In spite of this, key elements of democracy appear to be lacking in a number of pressure groups. How many groups genuinely offer the opportunity to participate in policy making? The concept of pressure-group competition on a level playing field is patently a false one, and the existence of a tightly closed 'insider' network ensures that only a small number of groups actually have any influence on the policy-making process. Unlike political parties, groups are not accountable to anyone, perhaps apart from their members. This gives them much greater freedom of action, with little political cost for failed campaigns or strategies.

To say that pressure groups are a threat to democracy is rather overstating the matter, as most groups have little interest in how the country is governed or in the rights of its citizens. Perhaps the biggest threat from pressure-group activity is the idea that merely setting up a direct debit for membership is an adequate substitute for participation in the political system.

Task 5.3

(a) Why might the possibility of accessing the political system at EU level appeal to some groups, but not to others?

(b) For what reasons might the European Commission encourage pressure-group activity in the EU?

Guidance

(a) To answer this question, you need to consider the kind of issues a group is concerned with. Is it one that has a multinational dimension (e.g. the environment)? Is it relevant to an area of EU policy competence (e.g. competition policy)? Does the group have the resources to staff an office in Brussels?

Task 5.3 (continued)

(b) The Commission actively encourages pressure-group activity because it partially compensates for the democratic deficit that exists within the EU. The Commission also relies on groups to act as whistle blowers on national governments that are failing to implement EU legislation. Groups can also be useful in facilitating the implementation of EU policy. The Commission also requires the detailed technical knowledge of policy that many groups can provide.

Useful websites

- Li, Y., Savage, M., Tampubolon, G., Warde, A. and Tomlinson, M. (2002) *Dynamics of Social Capital: Trends and Turnover in Associational Membership in England and Wales, 1972–1999*
  www.socresonline.org.uk/7/3/li.html
- The Fairtrade Foundation
  www.fairtrade.org.uk/

Further reading

- Garner, R. (2000) *Environmental Politics: Britain, Europe and the Global Environment*, 2nd edn, pp. 145–49.
- Maloney, W. (2002) 'Political participation beyond the electoral arena', in P. Dunleavy, R. Heffernan, P. Cowley and C. Hay (eds) *Developments in British Politics 8*, Palgrave Macmillan.

Glossary

cartel party

This is a recent development in party organisation. One theory is that parties have become increasingly 'professionalised' and remote from their members. In the process, they have come to rely heavily on the state for resources and have become dependent on the state.

catch-all party

A catch-all political party is a party or political movement that attracts a broad support base that often defies simple categorisation. It may contain supporters of different political creeds, to such an extent that in some cases supporters from each party can align themselves with a particular politician or group within the other. The Labour Party under Tony Blair is frequently held as an example of a catch-all party. Critics of catch-all parties accuse them of populism, adopting whichever policies they need to win, without any ideological conviction or clear definition.

cause group

A cause group is a pressure group whose members are united by particular issues. Cause groups generally have three objectives: reform the political system (e.g. Charter 88), challenge existing assumptions and attitudes (e.g. Friends of the Earth), or protect the vulnerable (Shelter/RSPB).

corporatism

This term describes the incorporation of organised interests, such as the business community and labour movement, into the policy process. Decision making in post-war Britain was loosely based on this model, with the Confederation of British Industry and Trades Union Congress regularly consulted about the management of the British economy.

direct action

Direct action is a form of political protest designed to generate interest in a cause among the general public. It rejects the use of insider strategies to influence policy making and focuses on an event that is likely to guarantee extensive media coverage. In recent years, it has become a widely used tactic of certain types of pressure group, usually either those that are rejected by the established political actors, or those that have no wish to be participants in the 'political game'.

electoral college

A device used by the Labour Party to elect its party leader, deputy leader and regional leaders. It consists of three sections, representing three different parts of the party. It gives the impression that each section of the party is equally represented, but it appears to be a device to maintain the supremacy of the parliamentary party in electing its leader.

Eurogroups

Pressure groups that wish to lobby at EU level frequently associate themselves with similar groups from other EU member states. Examples include Eurogroup for Animal Welfare and the Union of Industrial and Employers Confederation of Europe.

insider group

This is a group regarded as legitimate by government and consulted on a regular basis. It is usually a sectional group, such as the British Medical Association, but some cause groups, such as the Howard League for Penal Reform, have also achieved insider status. Grant subdivides insider groups into high-profile, low-profile or prisoner groups. Insider groups are often consulted because of their specialist knowledge of an area of policy and because they can often help with the implementation of policy.

mass party

This is a party organisation that aims to construct as broad a membership range as possible, in order to appeal to a wide section of the population. Power over policy making and the election of leaders is placed in the hands of the mass membership. Originally formed outside parliament, in contrast to the Conservative and Liberal parties, the Labour Party retained many of the characteristics of a mass party until the mid-1980s.

McKenzie's thesis

Robert McKenzie was a political scientist and broadcaster, arguably most famous for introducing the swingometer to television coverage of elections. His 1955 work, *British Political Parties: the Distribution of Power within the Conservative and Labour Parties* was a landmark text on the workings of British political parties and was hugely influential in describing the nature of the British party system. Its thesis was simple: only two parties mattered in British politics, something which was central to the workings of British democracy. One party wins and forms the government; the other does not win and acts as a powerful scrutiniser of government actions. By offering itself as a credible 'government-in-waiting' it also provides a choice to the electorate. His thesis was driven home by the fact that all but two pages of the book dealt with the two main parties.

new politics

This term refers to the emergence of a new, non-ideological consensus that is supposed to exist between the main parties. Parties emphasise their qualities according to levels of competence and their ability to manage the economy better than their rivals.

new social movement

This refers to a wave of social movements that differ from earlier social movements in focus and methods. Earlier movements were associated with economic gains (e.g. the trade unions), but the new wave was influenced by broader concerns: gender, the environment, peace. They are usually concerned with a narrower range of issues. New social movements place greater emphasis on influencing the culture of a society by appealing to the population, rather than relying on conventional methods of influence.

one member, one vote

This phrase describes a system of universal and equal voting, usually in the context of a political party's organisation.

outsider group

This is a group that does not have regular access to ministers or civil servants. Outsider groups can be subdivided into groups that wish to become insiders and those that have no wish to become insiders. The 'wannabes' often include aspirant and new groups, while those who have no wish to gain direct access hold such a position through either choice or necessity.

party system

The term 'party system' refers to the relationships both between and within political parties. It usually describes the number of parties that can reasonably be expected to hold some kind of power or political influence in a political system.

pluralism

A view of society in which decision making stems from competition between groups of more or less equal power, which is resolved by the victory of the group with the best ideas, and/or which is deemed to be most representative of public opinion. Supporters of this idea claim that no single group can gain dominance of the political system as no group possesses the resources or expertise to dominate several areas of policy.

post-war consensus

This is a term used to describe the broad agreement over the fundamental aspects of British politics. Both the major parties supported the idea of the NHS and the state's responsibility for tackling the root causes of inequality. Arguably, the most significant area of agreement was over the government's need to pursue Keynesian demand management policies in order to improve economic performance.

relevant parties

Giovanni Sartori argued that it was not enough to count the number of political parties that won seats after elections. In order to gauge what kind of party system a political system possessed, what mattered was how many parties could be said to be relevant. This idea has allowed academics to distinguish more precisely between party systems. There are different ways to determine relevance. Pippa Norris focuses on those parties who have won over 3% of the parliamentary seats; others choose a less generous figure. Sartori preferred to consider more contextual criteria.

sectional group

A sectional group is a pressure group that represents a particular section of society. Types of sectional group include trade unions, professional associations and those with a shared leisure or lifestyle background, such as motoring or disability groups.

social capital

Social capital can be defined as the links between people upon which trust and altruism are based. Social capital is built by people working closely with each other in their everyday lives or in a political context. Because of its emphasis on the importance of social cohesion and working together, it is regarded by some academics as central to the fabric of democracy.

The Third Way

A phrase commonly associated with Anthony Giddens or with Tony Blair before 1997. Routinely described as advocating a form of politics that rejected both unfettered market capitalism and statist interventionism, it emphasised the importance of individual freedoms, while insisting on the need for communities to work together to tackle society's problems.